The Revenge of Bussy D'Ambois by George Chapman

A TRAGEDIE

As it hath beene often presented at the priuate Play-house in the White Fryers.

George Chapman was born at Hitchin in Hertfordshire in about 1559. There is some evidence that Chapman attended Oxford University but did not obtain a degree, but the evidence is rather scant.

During the first part of the early 1590s Chapman was in Europe, in military action in the Low Countries fighting under the famed English general Sir Francis Vere.

It is from this period that his earliest published works are found including the obscure philosophical poems The Shadow of Night (1594) and Ovid's Banquet of Sense (1595).

By the end of the 1590s, Chapman had become a successful playwright, working for the Elizabethan Theatrical entrepreneur, Philip Henslowe, and later for the Children of the Chapel.

From 1598 he published his translation of the Iliad in installments. In 1616 the complete Iliad and Odyssey appeared in The Whole Works of Homer, the first complete English translation, which until Alexander Pope's, was the most popular in the English language and was the entry point for most English readers of these magnificent poems.

The great Ben Jonson was also using Chapman's talents in the play Eastward Ho (1605), co-written with John Marston. Both Chapman and Jonson landed in jail over some satirical references to the Scots in the play but both were quick to say that Marston was the culprit.

Chapman also wrote one of the most successful masques of the Jacobean era, The Memorable Masque of the Middle Temple and Lincoln's Inn, performed on February 15th, 1613. Another masque, The Masque of the Twelve Months, performed on Twelfth Night 1619 is also now given as Chapman's.

George Chapman died in London on May 12th, 1634 having lived his latter years in poverty and debt. He was buried at St Giles in the Fields.

Index of Contents

INTRODUCTION

The Revenge of Bussy D'Ambois was printed in quarto in 1613 by T. S. for John Helme. No reprint appeared till 1873, when it was included in the edition of Chapman's Tragedies and Comedies published by J. Pearson. The text of the quarto was reproduced, with the original spelling and punctuation, but with a few errors. There have been two later editions in modernized spelling, and with slight emendations, by R. H. Shepherd in 1874, and W. L. Phelps in 1895.

In the present edition the text of the quarto has been reproduced, with some additional emendations, and the original spelling has been retained. As regards punctuation, the use of capital letters and italics, and the division of the Acts into Scenes, the same methods have been followed as in the case of Bussy D'Ambois.

SOURCES

The story of a plot by Bussy D'Ambois's kinsfolk to avenge his murder is, in the main, of Chapman's own invention. But he had evidently read an account similar to that given later by De Thou of the design entertained for a time by Bussy's sister Renée (whom Chapman calls Charlotte) and her husband, Baligny, to take vengeance on Montsurry. Clermont D'Ambois is himself a fictitious character, but the episodes in which he appears in Acts II-IV are drawn from the account of the treacherous proceedings against the Count d'Auvergne in Edward Grimeston's translation of Jean de Serres's Inventaire Général de l'Histoire de France. This narrative, however, is not by De Serres, but by Pierre Matthieu, whose Histoire de France was one of the sources used by Grimeston for events later than 1598.

The portraiture of Clermont throughout the play as the high-souled philosopher is inspired by Epictetus's delineation in his Discourses of the ideal Stoic. But in his reluctance to carry out his duty of revenge he is evidently modelled upon Hamlet. In Act V, Scene i, the influence of Shakespeare's tragedy is specially manifest.

The Scenes in Act V relating to the assassination of Guise are based upon Grimeston's translation of De Serres's Inventaire Général.

The passages in Grimeston's volume which recount the Duke's murder, and those which tell the story of the Count d'Auvergne, are reprinted as an Appendix.

TO THE RIGHT VERTUOUS, AND truely Noble Knight, Sr. Thomas Howard, &c.

Sir,

Since workes of this kinde have beene lately esteemed worthy the patronage of some of our worthiest Nobles, I have made no doubt to preferre this of mine to your undoubted vertue and exceeding true noblesse, as contayning matter no lesse deserving your reading, and excitation to heroycall life, then any such late dedication. Nor have the greatest Princes of Italie and other countries conceived it any least diminution to their greatnesse to have their names wing'd with these tragicke plumes, and disperst by way of patronage through the most noble notices of Europe.

Howsoever, therefore, in the scænicall presentation it might meete with some maligners, yet, considering even therein it past with approbation of more worthy judgements, the ballance of their side (especially being held by your impartiall hand) I hope will to no graine abide the out-weighing. And for the autenticall truth of eyther person or action, who (worth the respecting) will expect it in a poeme, whose subject is not truth, but things like truth? Poore envious soules they are that cavill at truths want in these naturall fictions: materiall instruction, elegant and sententious excitation to vertue, and deflection from her contrary, being the soule, lims, and limits of an autenticall tragedie. But whatsoever merit of your full countenance and favour suffers defect in this, I shall soone supply with some other of more generall account; wherein your right vertuous name made famous and preserved to posteritie, your future comfort and honour in your present acceptation and love of all vertuous and divine expression may be so much past others of your rancke encreast, as they are short of your judiciall ingenuitie, in their due estimation.

For howsoever those ignoble and sowre-brow'd worldlings are carelesse of whatsoever future or present opinion spreads of them; yet (with the most divine philosopher, if Scripture did not confirme it) I make it matter of my faith, that we truely retaine an intellectuall feeling of good or bad after this life, proportionably answerable to the love or neglect we beare here to all vertue and truely-humane instruction: in whose favour and honour I wish you most eminent, and rest ever,

Your true vertues
most true observer,

George Chapman.

DRAMATIS PERSONAE

Henry, the King.
Monsieur, his Brother.
Guise, Duke.
Renel, a Marquesse.
Montsurry, an Earle.
Baligny, Lord Lieutenant of Cambrai.
Clermont D'Ambois.
Maillard   }
Challon.   } Captaines.
Aumal.   }
Espernone.
Soissone.
Perricot, An Usher.
A Messenger.
The Guard.
Souldiers.
Servants.

                        {Bussy.
                        {Monsieur.
The ghosts of   {Guise.
                        {Card. Guise.
                        {Shattilion.

Countess of Cambrai.
Tamyra, wife to Montsureau.
Charlotte D'Ambois, wife to Baligny.
Riova, a Servant to the Countesse.

SCENE - Paris, and in or near Cambrai

The Revenge of Bussy D'Ambois. A Tragedie

ACTUS PRIMI

SCÆNA PRIMA

A Room at the Court in Paris

Enter **BALIGNY, RENEL**.

BALIGNY

To what will this declining kingdome turne,
Swindging in every license, as in this
Stupide permission of brave D'Ambois Murther?
Murther made paralell with Law! Murther us'd
To serve the kingdome, given by sute to men
For their advancement! suffered scarcrow-like
To fright adulterie! what will policie
At length bring under his capacitie?

RENEL

All things; for as, when the high births of Kings,
Deliverances, and coronations,
We celebrate with all the cities bels
Jangling together in untun'd confusion,
All order'd clockes are tyed up; so, when glory,
Flatterie, and smooth applauses of things ill,
Uphold th'inordinate swindge of downe-right power,
Justice, and truth that tell the bounded use,
Vertuous and well distinguisht formes of time,
Are gag'd and tongue-tide. But wee have observ'd
Rule in more regular motion: things most lawfull
Were once most royall; Kings sought common good,
Mens manly liberties, though ne'er so meane,
And had their owne swindge so more free, and more.
But when pride enter'd them, and rule by power,
All browes that smil'd beneath them, frown'd; hearts griev'd
By imitation; vertue quite was vanisht,
And all men studi'd selfe-love, fraud, and vice.
Then no man could be good but he was punisht.
Tyrants, being still more fearefull of the good
Then of the bad, their subjects vertues ever
Manag'd with curbs and dangers, and esteem'd
As shadowes and detractions to their owne.

BALIGNY

Now all is peace, no danger, now what followes?
Idlenesse rusts us, since no vertuous labour
Ends ought rewarded; ease, securitie,
Now all the palme weares. Wee made warre before
So to prevent warre; men with giving gifts,
More then receiving, made our countrey strong;
Our matchlesse race of souldiers then would spend
In publike warres, not private brawles, their spirits;

In daring enemies, arm'd with meanest armes,
Not courting strumpets, and consuming birth-rights
In apishnesse and envy of attire.
No labour then was harsh, no way so deepe,
No rocke so steepe, but if a bird could scale it,
Up would our youth flie to. A foe in armes
Stirr'd up a much more lust of his encounter
Then of a mistresse never so be-painted.
Ambition then was onely scaling walles,
And over-topping turrets; fame was wealth;
Best parts, best deedes, were best nobilitie;
Honour with worth, and wealth well got or none.
Countries we wonne with as few men as countries:
Vertue subdu'd all.

RENEL
Just: and then our nobles
Lov'd vertue so, they prais'd and us'd it to;
Had rather doe then say; their owne deedes hearing
By others glorified, then be so barraine
That their parts onely stood in praising others.

BALIGNY
Who could not doe, yet prais'd, and envi'd not;
Civile behaviour flourisht; bountie flow'd;
Avarice to upland boores, slaves, hang-men banisht.

RENEL
Tis now quite otherwise. But to note the cause
Of all these foule digressions and revolts
From our first natures, this tis in a word:
Since good arts faile, crafts and deceits are us'd:
Men ignorant are idle; idle men
Most practise what they most may doe with ease,
Fashion and favour; all their studies ayming
At getting money, which no wise man ever
Fed his desires with.

BALIGNY
Yet now none are wise
That thinke not heavens true foolish, weigh'd with that.
Well, thou most worthy to be greatest Guise,
Make with thy greatnesse a new world arise.
Such deprest nobles (followers of his)
As you, my selfe, my lord, will finde a time
When to revenge your wrongs.

RENEL

I make no doubt:
In meane time, I could wish the wrong were righted
Of your slaine brother in law, brave Bussy D'Ambois.

BALIGNY
That one accident was made my charge.
My brother Bussy's sister (now my wife)
By no suite would consent to satisfie
My love of her with marriage, till I vow'd
To use my utmost to revenge my brother:
But Clermont D'Ambois (*Bussy's second brother*)
Had, since, his apparition, and excitement
To suffer none but his hand in his wreake;
Which hee hath vow'd, and so will needes acquite
Me of my vow made to my wife, his sister,
And undertake himselfe Bussy's revenge.
Yet loathing any way to give it act,
But in the noblest and most manly course,
If th'Earle dares take it, he resolves to send
A challenge to him, and my selfe must beare it;
To which deliverie I can use no meanes,
He is so barricado'd in his house,
And arm'd with guard still.

RENEL
That meanes lay on mee,
Which I can strangely make. My last lands sale,
By his great suite, stands now on price with him,
And hee (as you know) passing covetous,
With that blinde greedinesse that followes gaine,
Will cast no danger where her sweete feete tread.
Besides, you know, his lady, by his suite
(Wooing as freshly as when first love shot
His faultlesse arrowes from her rosie eyes)
Now lives with him againe, and shee, I know,
Will joyne with all helps in her friends revenge.

BALIGNY
No doubt, my lord, and therefore let me pray you
To use all speede; for so on needels points
My wifes heart stands with haste of the revenge,
Being (as you know) full of her brothers fire,
That shee imagines I neglect my vow;
Keepes off her kinde embraces, and still askes,
"When, when, will this revenge come? when perform'd
Will this dull vow be?" And, I vow to heaven,
So sternely, and so past her sexe she urges
My vowes performance, that I almost feare

To see her, when I have a while beene absent,
Not showing her, before I speake, the bloud
She so much thirsts for, freckling hands and face.

RENEL
Get you the challenge writ, and looke from me
To heare your passage clear'd no long time after.

[Exit **RENEL**.

BALIGNY
All restitution to your worthiest lordship!
Whose errand I must carrie to the King,
As having sworne my service in the search
Of all such malecontents and their designes,
By seeming one affected with their faction
And discontented humours gainst the state:
Nor doth my brother Clermont scape my counsaile
Given to the King about his Guisean greatnesse,
Which (as I spice it) hath possest the King,
Knowing his daring spirit, of much danger
Charg'd in it to his person; though my conscience
Dare sweare him cleare of any power to be
Infected with the least dishonestie:
Yet that sinceritie, wee politicians
Must say, growes out of envie since it cannot
Aspire to policies greatnesse; and the more
We worke on all respects of kinde and vertue,
The more our service to the King seemes great,
In sparing no good that seemes bad to him:
And the more bad we make the most of good,
The more our policie searcheth, and our service
Is wonder'd at for wisedome and sincerenesse.
Tis easie to make good suspected still,
Where good, and God, are made but cloakes for ill.

[Enter **HENRY, MONSIEUR, GUISE, CLERMONT D'AMBOIS, ESPERONE, SOISSONE. MONSIEUR** taking
leave of the **KING**.

See Monsieur taking now his leave for Brabant;
The Guise & his deare minion, Clermont D'Ambois,
Whispering together, not of state affaires,
I durst lay wagers, (though the Guise be now
In chiefe heate of his faction) but of some thing
Savouring of that which all men else despise,
How to be truely noble, truely wise.

MONSIEUR

See how hee hangs upon the eare of Guise,
Like to his jewell!

EPERON
Hee's now whisp'ring in
Some doctrine of stabilitie and freedome,
Contempt of outward greatnesse, and the guises
That vulgar great ones make their pride and zeale,
Being onely servile traines, and sumptuous houses,
High places, offices.

MONSIEUR
Contempt of these
Does he read to the Guise? Tis passing needfull,
And hee, I thinke, makes show t'affect his doctrine.

EPERON
Commends, admires it—

MONSIEUR
And pursues another.
Tis fine hypocrisie, and cheape, and vulgar,
Knowne for a covert practise, yet beleev'd
By those abus'd soules that they teach and governe
No more then wives adulteries by their husbands,
They bearing it with so unmov'd aspects,
Hot comming from it, as twere not at all,
Or made by custome nothing. This same D'Ambois
Hath gotten such opinion of his vertues,
Holding all learning but an art to live well,
And showing hee hath learn'd it in his life,
Being thereby strong in his perswading others,
That this ambitious Guise, embracing him,
Is thought t'embrace his vertues.

EPERON
Yet in some
His vertues are held false for th'others vices:
For tis more cunning held, and much more common,
To suspect truth then falshood: and of both
Truth still fares worse, as hardly being beleev'd,
As tis unusuall and rarely knowne.

MONSIEUR
Ile part engendring vertue. Men affirme,
Though this same Clermont hath a D'Ambois spirit,
And breathes his brothers valour, yet his temper
Is so much past his that you cannot move him:

Ile try that temper in him.—Come, you two
Devoure each other with your vertues zeale,
And leave for other friends no fragment of yee:
I wonder, Guise, you will thus ravish him
Out of my bosome, that first gave the life
His manhood breathes spirit, and meanes, and luster.
What doe men thinke of me, I pray thee, Clermont?
Once give me leave (for tryall of that love
That from thy brother Bussy thou inherit'st)
T'unclaspe thy bosome.

CLERMONT
As how, sir?

MONSIEUR
Be a true glasse to mee, in which I may
Behold what thoughts the many-headed beast
And thou thy selfe breathes out concerning me,
My ends and new upstarted state in Brabant,
For which I now am bound, my higher aymes
Imagin'd here in France: speake, man, and let
Thy words be borne as naked as thy thoughts.
O were brave Bussy living!

CLERMONT
Living, my lord!

MONSIEUR
Tis true thou art his brother, but durst thou
Have brav'd the Guise; mauger his presence, courted
His wedded lady; emptied even the dregs
Of his worst thoughts of mee even to my teeth;
Discern'd not me, his rising soveraigne,
From any common groome, but let me heare
My grossest faults, as grosse-full as they were?
Durst thou doe this?

CLERMONT
I cannot tell. A man
Does never know the goodnesse of his stomacke
Till hee sees meate before him. Were I dar'd,
Perhaps, as he was, I durst doe like him.

MONSIEUR
Dare then to poure out here thy freest soule
Of what I am.

CLERMONT

Tis stale, he tolde you it.

MONSIEUR
He onely jested, spake of splene and envie;
Thy soule, more learn'd, is more ingenuous,
Searching, judiciall; let me then from thee
Heare what I am.

CLERMONT
What but the sole support,
And most expectant hope of all our France,
The toward victor of the whole Low Countryes?

MONSIEUR
Tush, thou wilt sing encomions of my praise!
Is this like D'Ambois? I must vexe the Guise,
Or never looke to heare free truth. Tell me,
For Bussy lives not; hee durst anger mee,
Yet, for my love, would not have fear'd to anger
The King himselfe. Thou understand'st me, dost not?

CLERMONT
I shall my lord, with studie.

MONSIEUR
Dost understand thy selfe? I pray thee tell me,
Dost never search thy thoughts, what my designe
Might be to entertaine thee and thy brother?
What turne I meant to serve with you?

CLERMONT
Even what you please to thinke.

MONSIEUR
But what thinkst thou?
Had I no end in't, think'st?

CLERMONT
I thinke you had.

MONSIEUR
When I tooke in such two as you two were,
A ragged couple of decaid commanders,
When a French-crowne would plentifully serve
To buy you both to any thing i'th'earth—

CLERMONT
So it would you.

MONSIEUR

Nay bought you both out-right,
You and your trunkes—I feare me, I offend thee.

CLERMONT

No, not a jot.

MONSIEUR

The most renowmed souldier,
Epaminondas (as good authors say)
Had no more suites then backes, but you two shar'd
But one suite twixt you both, when both your studies
Were not what meate to dine with, if your partridge,
Your snipe, your wood-cocke, larke, or your red hering,
But where to begge it; whether at my house,
Or at the Guises (for you know you were
Ambitious beggars) or at some cookes-shop,
T'eternize the cookes trust, and score it up.
Dost not offend thee?

CLERMONT

No, sir. Pray proceede.

MONSIEUR

As for thy gentry, I dare boldly take
Thy honourable othe: and yet some say
Thou and thy most renowmed noble brother
Came to the Court first in a keele of sea-coale.
Dost not offend thee?

CLERMONT

Never doubt it, sir.

MONSIEUR

Why doe I love thee, then? Why have I rak'd thee
Out of the dung-hill? cast my cast ward-robe on thee?
Brought thee to Court to, as I did thy brother?
Made yee my sawcy bon companions?
Taught yee to call our greatest Noblemen
By the corruption of their names—Jack, Tom?
Have I blowne both for nothing to this bubble?
Though thou art learn'd, thast no enchanting wit;
Or, were thy wit good, am I therefore bound
To keepe thee for my table?

CLERMONT

Well, sir, 'twere

A good knights place. Many a proud dubb'd gallant
Seekes out a poore knights living from such emrods.

MONSIEUR
Or what use else should I designe thee to?
Perhaps you'll answere me—to be my pander.

CLERMONT
Perhaps I shall.

MONSIEUR
Or did the slie Guise put thee
Into my bosome t'undermine my projects?
I feare thee not; for, though I be not sure
I have thy heart, I know thy braine-pan yet
To be as emptie a dull piece of wainscot
As ever arm'd the scalpe of any courtier;
A fellow onely that consists of sinewes;
Meere Swisser, apt for any execution.

CLERMONT
But killing of the King!

MONSIEUR
Right: now I see
Thou understand'st thy selfe.

CLERMONT
I, and you better.
You are a Kings sonne borne.

MONSIEUR
Right.

CLERMONT
And a Kings brother.

MONSIEUR
True.

CLERMONT
And might not any foole have beene so too,
As well as you?

MONSIEUR
A poxe upon you!

CLERMONT

You did no princely deedes
Ere you were borne (I take it) to deserve it;
Nor did you any since that I have heard;
Nor will doe ever any, as all thinke.

MONSIEUR
The Divell take him! Ile no more of him.

GUISE
Nay: stay, my lord, and heare him answere you.

MONSIEUR
No more, I sweare. Farewell.

[Exeunt **MONSIEUR, ESPERONE, SOISSONE.**

GUISE
No more! Ill fortune!
I would have given a million to have heard
His scoffes retorted, and the insolence
Of his high birth and greatnesse (which were never
Effects of his deserts, but of his fortune)
Made show to his dull eyes beneath the worth
That men aspire to by their knowing vertues,
Without which greatnesse is a shade, a bubble.

CLERMONT
But what one great man dreames of that but you?
All take their births and birth-rights left to them
(Acquir'd by others) for their owne worths purchase,
When many a foole in both is great as they:
And who would thinke they could winne with their worths
Wealthy possessions, when, wonne to their hands,
They neyther can judge justly of their value,
Nor know their use? and therefore they are puft
With such proud tumours as this Monsieur is,
Enabled onely by the goods they have
To scorne all goodnesse: none great fill their fortunes;
But as those men that make their houses greater,
Their housholds being lesse, so Fortune raises
Huge heapes of out-side in these mightie men,
And gives them nothing in them.

GUISE
True as truth:
And therefore they had rather drowne their substance
In superfluities of brickes and stones
(Like Sysiphus, advancing of them ever,

And ever pulling downe) then lay the cost
Of any sluttish corner on a man,
Built with Gods finger, and enstil'd his temple.

BALIGNY
Tis nobly said, my lord.

GUISE
I would have these things
Brought upon stages, to let mightie misers
See all their grave and serious miseries plaid,
As once they were in Athens and olde Rome.

CLERMONT
Nay, we must now have nothing brought on stages,
But puppetry, and pide ridiculous antickes:
Men thither come to laugh, and feede fool-fat,
Checke at all goodnesse there, as being prophan'd:
When, wheresoever goodnesse comes, shee makes
The place still sacred, though with other feete
Never so much tis scandal'd and polluted.
Let me learne anything that fits a man,
In any stables showne, as well as stages.

BALIGNY
Why, is not all the world esteem'd a stage?

CLERMONT
Yes, and right worthily; and stages too
Have a respect due to them, if but onely
For what the good Greeke moralist sayes of them:
"Is a man proud of greatnesse, or of riches?
Give me an expert actor, Ile shew all,
That can within his greatest glory fall.
Is a man fraid with povertie and lownesse?
Give me an actor, Ile shew every eye
What hee laments so, and so much doth flye,
The best and worst of both." If but for this then,
To make the proudest out-side that most swels
With things without him, and above his worth,
See how small cause hee has to be so blowne up;
And the most poore man, to be griev'd with poorenesse,
Both being so easily borne by expert actors,
The stage and actors are not so contemptfull
As every innovating Puritane,
And ignorant sweater out of zealous envie
Would have the world imagine. And besides
That all things have been likened to the mirth

Us'd upon stages, and for stages fitted,
The splenative philosopher, that ever
Laught at them all, were worthy the enstaging.
All objects, were they ne'er so full of teares,
He so conceited that he could distill thence
Matter that still fed his ridiculous humour.
Heard he a lawyer, never so vehement pleading,
Hee stood and laught. Heard hee a trades-man swearing,
Never so thriftily selling of his wares,
He stood and laught. Heard hee an holy brother,
For hollow ostentation, at his prayers
Ne'er so impetuously, hee stood and laught.
Saw hee a great man never so insulting,
Severely inflicting, gravely giving lawes,
Not for their good, but his, hee stood and laught.
Saw hee a youthfull widow
Never so weeping, wringing of her hands
For her lost lord, still the philosopher laught.
Now whether hee suppos'd all these presentments
Were onely maskeries, and wore false faces,
Or else were simply vaine, I take no care;
But still hee laught, how grave soere they were.

GUISE
And might right well, my Clermont; and for this
Vertuous digression we will thanke the scoffes
Of vicious Monsieur. But now for the maine point
Of your late resolution for revenge
Of your slaine friend.

CLERMONT
I have here my challenge,
Which I will pray my brother Baligny
To beare the murtherous Earle.

BALIGNY
I have prepar'd
Meanes for accesse to him, through all his guard.

GUISE
About it then, my worthy Baligny,
And bring us the successe.

BALIGNY
I will, my lord.

[Exeunt.

A Room in Montsurry's House

TAMYRA sola.

TAMYRA
Revenge, that ever red sitt'st in the eyes
Of injur'd ladies, till we crowne thy browes
With bloudy lawrell, and receive from thee
Justice for all our honours injurie;
Whose wings none flye that wrath or tyrannie
Have ruthlesse made and bloudy, enter here,
Enter, O enter! and, though length of time
Never lets any scape thy constant justice,
Yet now prevent that length. Flye, flye, and here
Fixe thy steele foot-steps; here, O here, where still
Earth (mov'd with pittie) yeelded and embrac'd
My loves faire figure, drawne in his deare bloud,
And mark'd the place, to show thee where was done
The cruell'st murther that ere fled the sunne.
O Earth! why keep'st thou not as well his spirit,
To give his forme life? No, that was not earthly;
That (rarefying the thinne and yeelding ayre)
Flew sparkling up into the sphære of fire
Whence endlesse flames it sheds in my desire.
Here be my daily pallet; here all nights
That can be wrested from thy rivals armes,
O my deare Bussy, I will lye, and kisse
Spirit into thy bloud, or breathe out mine
In sighes, and kisses, and sad tunes to thine.

[She sings.

[Enter **MONTSURRY**.

MONTSURRY
Still on this hant? Still shall adulterous bloud
Affect thy spirits? Thinke, for shame, but this,
This bloud, that cockatrice-like thus thou brood'st,
To dry is to breede any quench to thine.
And therefore now (if onely for thy lust
A little cover'd with a vaile of shame)
Looke out for fresh life, rather then witch-like
Learne to kisse horror, and with death engender.
Strange crosse in nature, purest virgine shame

Lies in the bloud as lust lyes; and together
Many times mixe too; and in none more shamefull
Then in the shamefac't. Who can then distinguish
Twixt their affections; or tell when hee meetes
With one not common? Yet, as worthiest poets
Shunne common and plebeian formes of speech,
Every illiberall and affected phrase,
To clothe their matter, and together tye
Matter and forme with art and decencie;
So worthiest women should shunne vulgar guises,
And though they cannot but flye out for change,
Yet modestie, the matter of their lives,
Be it adulterate, should be painted true
With modest out-parts; what they should doe still
Grac'd with good show, though deedes be ne'er so ill.

TAMYRA
That is so farre from all yee seeke of us
That (though your selves be common as the ayre)
We must not take the ayre, wee must not fit
Our actions to our owne affections:
But as geometricians (you still say)
Teach that no lines, nor superficies,
Doe move themselves, but still accompanie
The motions of their bodies; so poore wives
Must not pursue, nor have their owne affections,
But to their husbands earnests, and their jests,
To their austerities of lookes, and laughters,
(Though ne'er so foolish and injurious)
Like parasites and slaves, fit their disposures.

MONTSURRY
I usde thee as my soule, to move and rule me.

TAMYRA
So said you, when you woo'd. So souldiers tortur'd
With tedious sieges of some wel-wall'd towne,
Propound conditions of most large contents,
Freedome of lawes, all former government;
But having once set foote within the wals,
And got the reynes of power into their hands,
Then doe they tyrannize at their owne rude swindges,
Seaze all their goods, their liberties, and lives,
And make advantage, and their lusts, their lawes.

MONTSURRY
But love me, and performe a wifes part yet,
With all my love before, I sweare forgivenesse.

TAMYRA

Forgivenesse! that grace you should seeke of mee:
These tortur'd fingers and these stab'd-through armes
Keepe that law in their wounds yet unobserv'd,
And ever shall.

MONTSURRY

Remember their deserts.

TAMYRA

Those with faire warnings might have beene reform'd,
Not these unmanly rages. You have heard
The fiction of the north winde and the sunne,
Both working on a traveller, and contending
Which had most power to take his cloake from him:
Which when the winde attempted, hee roar'd out
Outragious blasts at him to force it off,
That wrapt it closer on: when the calme sunne
(The winde once leaving) charg'd him with still beames,
Quiet and fervent, and therein was constant,
Which made him cast off both his cloake and coate;
Like whom should men doe. If yee wish your wives
Should leave dislik'd things, seeke it not with rage,
For that enrages; what yee give, yee have:
But use calme warnings, and kinde manly meanes,
And that in wives most prostitute will winne
Not onely sure amends, but make us wives
Better then those that ne'er led faultie lives.

[Enter a **SOLDIER**.

SOLDIER.

My lord.

MONTSURRY

How now; would any speake with me?

SOLDIER.

I, sir.

MONTSURRY

Perverse, and traiterous miscreant!
Where are your other fellowes of my guard?
Have I not told you I will speake with none
But Lord Renel?

SOLDIER

And it is hee that stayes you.

MONTSURRY
O, is it he? Tis well: attend him in.

[Exit **SOLDIER**.

I must be vigilant; the Furies haunt mee.
Doe you heare, dame?

[Enter **RENEL**, with the **SOLDIER**.

RENEL [Aside, to the **SOLDIER**].
Be true now, for your ladies injur'd sake,
Whose bountie you have so much cause to honour:
For her respect is chiefe in this designe,
And therefore serve it; call out of the way
All your confederate fellowes of his guard,
Till Monsieur Baligny be enter'd here.

SOLDIER
Upon your honour, my lord shall be free
From any hurt, you say?

RENEL
Free as my selfe. Watch then, and cleare his entrie.

SOLDIER
I will not faile, my lord.

[Exit **SOLDIER**.

RENEL
God save your lordship!

MONTSURRY
My noblest Lord Renel! past all men welcome!
Wife, welcome his lordship.

RENEL [To **TAMYRA**]
I much joy In your returne here.

TAMYRA
You doe more then I.

MONTSURRY
Shee's passionate still, to thinke we ever parted
By my too sterne injurious jelousie.

RENEL
Tis well your lordship will confesse your errour
In so good time yet.

[Enter **BALIGNY**, with a challenge.

MONTSURRY
Death! who have wee here?
Ho! Guard! Villaines!

BALIGNY
Why exclaime you so?

MONTSURRY
Negligent trayters! Murther, murther, murther!

BALIGNY
Y'are mad. Had mine entent beene so, like yours,
It had beene done ere this.

RENEL
Sir, your intent,
And action too, was rude to enter thus.

BALIGNY
Y'are a decaid lord to tell me of rudenesse,
As much decaid in manners as in meanes.

RENEL
You talke of manners, that thus rudely thrust
Upon a man that's busie with his wife!

BALIGNY
And kept your lordship then the dore?

RENEL
The dore!

MONTSURRY
Sweet lord, forbeare. Show, show your purpose, sir,
To move such bold feete into others roofes.

BALIGNY
This is my purpose, sir; from Clermont D'Ambois
I bring this challenge.

MONTSURRY

Challenge! Ile touch none.

BALIGNY
Ile leave it here then.

RENEL
Thou shall leave thy life first.

MONTSURRY
Murther, murther!

RENEL
Retire, my lord; get off.

[They all fight and **BALIGNY** drives in **MONTSURRY**.

Hold, or thy death shall hold thee. Hence, my lord!

BALIGNY
There lye the chalenge.

[Exit **MONTSURRY**.

RENEL
Was not this well handled?

BALIGNY
Nobly, my lord. All thankes.

[Exit **BALIGNY**.

TAMYRA
Ile make him reade it.

[Exit **TAMYRA**.

RENEL
This was a sleight well maskt. O what is man,
Unlesse he be a politician!

[Exit.

ACTUS SECUNDI

SCÆNA PRIMA

A Room at the Court

HENRY, BALIGNY.

HENRY
Come, Baligny, we now are private; say,
What service bring'st thou? make it short; the Guise
(Whose friend thou seem'st) is now in Court, and neare,
And may observe us.

BALIGNY
This, sir, then, in short.
The faction of the Guise (with which my policie,
For service to your Highnesse, seemes to joyne)
Growes ripe, and must be gather'd into hold;
Of which my brother Clermont being a part
Exceeding capitall, deserves to have
A capitall eye on him. And (as you may
With best advantage, and your speediest charge)
Command his apprehension: which (because
The Court, you know, is strong in his defence)
Wee must aske country swindge and open fields.
And therefore I have wrought him to goe downe
To Cambray with me (of which government
Your Highnesse bountie made mee your lieutenant),
Where when I have him, I will leave my house,
And faine some service out about the confines;
When, in the meane time, if you please to give
Command to my lieutenant, by your letters,
To traine him to some muster, where he may
(Much to his honour) see for him your forces
Put into battaile, when hee comes, hee may
With some close stratageme be apprehended:
For otherwise your whole powers there will faile
To worke his apprehension: and with that
My hand needes never be discern'd therein.

HENRY
Thankes, honest Baligny.

BALIGNY
Your Highnesse knowes
I will be honest, and betray for you
Brother and father; for I know (my lord)
Treacherie for Kings is truest loyaltie,
Nor is to beare the name of treacherie,
But grave, deepe policie. All acts that seeme
Ill in particular respects are good

As they respect your universal rule:
As in the maine sway of the Universe
The supreame Rectors generall decrees,
To guard the mightie globes of earth and heaven,
Since they make good that guard to preservation
Of both those in their order and first end,
No mans particular (as hee thinkes) wrong
Must hold him wrong'd; no, not though all mens reasons,
All law, all conscience, concludes it wrong.
Nor is comparison a flatterer
To liken you here to the King of Kings;
Nor any mans particular offence
Against the worlds sway, to offence at yours
In any subject; who as little may
Grudge at their particular wrong, if so it seeme
For th'universall right of your estate,
As, being a subject of the worlds whole sway
As well as yours, and being a righteous man
To whom heaven promises defence, and blessing,
Brought to decay, disgrace, and quite defencelesse,
Hee may complaine of heaven for wrong to him.

HENRY
Tis true: the simile at all parts holds,
As all good subjects hold, that love our favour.

BALIGNY
Which is our heaven here; and a miserie
Incomparable, and most truely hellish,
To live depriv'd of our Kings grace and countenance,
Without which best conditions are most cursed:
Life of that nature, howsoever short,
Is a most lingering and tedious life;
Or rather no life, but a languishing,
And an abuse of life.

HENRY
Tis well conceited.

BALIGNY
I thought it not amisse to yeeld your Highness
A reason of my speeches; lest perhaps
You might conceive I flatter'd: which (I know)
Of all ils under heaven you most abhorre.

HENRY
Still thou art right, my vertuous Baligny,
For which I thanke and love thee. Thy advise

Ile not forget. Haste to thy government,
And carry D'Ambois with thee. So farewell.

[Exit.

BALIGNY
Your Majestie fare ever like it selfe.

[Enter **GUISE**.

GUISE
My sure friend Baligny!

BALIGNY
Noblest of princes!

GUISE
How stands the state of Cambray?

BALIGNY
Strong, my lord,
And fit for service: for whose readinesse
Your creature, Clermont D'Ambois, and my selfe
Ride shortly downe.

GUISE
That Clermont is my love;
France never bred a nobler gentleman
For all parts; he exceeds his brother Bussy.

BALIGNY
I, my lord?

GUISE
Farre: because (besides his valour)
Hee hath the crowne of man and all his parts,
Which Learning is; and that so true and vertuous
That it gives power to doe as well as say
What ever fits a most accomplisht man;
Which Bussy, for his valours season, lackt;
And so was rapt with outrage oftentimes
Beyond decorum; where this absolute Clermont,
Though (onely for his naturall zeale to right)
Hee will be fiery, when hee sees it crost,
And in defence of it, yet when he lists
Hee can containe that fire, as hid in embers.

BALIGNY

No question, hee's a true, learn'd gentleman.

GUISE
He is as true as tides, or any starre
Is in his motion; and for his rare learning,
Hee is not (as all else are that seeke knowledge)
Of taste so much deprav'd that they had rather
Delight and satisfie themselves to drinke
Of the streame troubled, wandring ne'er so farre
From the cleare fount, then of the fount it selfe.
In all, Romes Brutus is reviv'd in him,
Whom hee of industry doth imitate;
Or rather, as great Troys Euphorbus was
After Pithagoras, so is Brutus, Clermont.
And, were not Brutus a conspirator—

BALIGNY
Conspirator, my lord! Doth that empaire him?
Cæsar beganne to tyrannize; and when vertue,
Nor the religion of the Gods, could serve
To curbe the insolence of his proud lawes,
Brutus would be the Gods just instrument.
What said the Princesse, sweet Antigone,
In the grave Greeke tragedian, when the question
Twixt her and Creon is for lawes of Kings?
Which when he urges, shee replies on him
Though his lawes were a Kings, they were not Gods;
Nor would shee value Creons written lawes
With Gods unwrit edicts, since they last not
This day and the next, but every day and ever,
Where Kings lawes alter every day and houre,
And in that change imply a bounded power.

GUISE
Well, let us leave these vaine disputings what
Is to be done, and fall to doing something.
When are you for your government in Cambray?

BALIGNY
When you command, my lord.

GUISE
Nay, that's not fit.
Continue your designements with the King,
With all your service; onely, if I send,
Respect me as your friend, and love my Clermont.

BALIGNY

Your Highnesse knowes my vowes.

GUISE
I, tis enough.

[Exit **GUISE**. Manet **BALIGNY**.

BALIGNY
Thus must wee play on both sides, and thus harten
In any ill those men whose good wee hate.
Kings may doe what they list, and for Kings, subjects,
Eyther exempt from censure or exception;
For, as no mans worth can be justly judg'd
But when he shines in some authoritie,
So no authoritie should suffer censure
But by a man of more authoritie.
Great vessels into lesse are emptied never,
There's a redoundance past their continent ever.
These virtuosi are the poorest creatures;
For looke how spinners weave out of themselves
Webs, whose strange matter none before can see;
So these, out of an unseene good in vertue,
Make arguments of right and comfort in her,
That clothe them like the poore web of a spinner.

[Enter **CLERMONT**.

CLERMONT
Now, to my challenge. What's the place, the weapon?

BALIGNY
Soft, sir! let first your challenge be received.
Hee would not touch, nor see it.

CLERMONT
Possible!
How did you then?

BALIGNY
Left it, in his despight.
But when hee saw mee enter so expectlesse,
To heare his base exclaimes of "murther, murther,"
Made mee thinke noblesse lost, in him quicke buried.

CLERMONT
They are the breathing sepulchres of noblesse:
No trulier noble men then lions pictures,
Hung up for signes, are lions. Who knowes not

That lyons the more soft kept, are more servile?
And looke how lyons close kept, fed by hand,
Lose quite th'innative fire of spirit and greatnesse
That lyons free breathe, forraging for prey,
And grow so grosse that mastifes, curs, and mungrils
Have spirit to cow them: so our soft French Nobles
Chain'd up in ease and numbd securitie
(Their spirits shrunke up like their covetous fists,
And never opened but Domitian-like,
And all his base, obsequious minions
When they were catching though it were but flyes),
Besotted with their pezzants love of gaine,
Rusting at home, and on each other preying,
Are for their greatnesse but the greater slaves,
And none is noble but who scrapes and saves.

BALIGNY
Tis base, tis base; and yet they thinke them high.

CLERMONT
So children mounted on their hobby-horse
Thinke they are riding, when with wanton toile
They beare what should beare them. A man may well
Compare them to those foolish great-spleen'd cammels,
That to their high heads beg'd of Jove hornes higher;
Whose most uncomely and ridiculous pride
When hee had satisfied, they could not use,
But where they went upright before, they stoopt,
And bore their heads much lower for their hornes:
As these high men doe, low in all true grace,
Their height being priviledge to all things base.
And as the foolish poet that still writ
All his most selfe-lov'd verse in paper royall,
Or partchment rul'd with lead, smooth'd with the pumice,
Bound richly up, and strung with crimson strings;
Never so blest as when hee writ and read
The ape-lov'd issue of his braine; and never
But joying in himselfe, admiring ever:
Yet in his workes behold him, and hee show'd
Like to a ditcher. So these painted men,
All set on out-side, looke upon within,
And not a pezzants entrailes you shall finde
More foule and mezel'd, nor more sterv'd of minde.

BALIGNY
That makes their bodies fat. I faine would know
How many millions of our other Nobles
Would make one Guise. There is a true tenth Worthy,

Who, did not one act onely blemish him—

CLERMONT
One act! what one?

BALIGNY
One that though yeeres past done
Stickes by him still, and will distaine him ever.

CLERMONT
Good heaven! wherein? what one act can you name
Suppos'd his staine that Ile not prove his luster?

BALIGNY
To satisfie you, twas the Massacre.

CLERMONT
The Massacre! I thought twas some such blemish.

BALIGNY
O, it was hainous!

CLERMONT
To a brutish sense,
But not a manly reason. Wee so tender
The vile part in us that the part divine
We see in hell, and shrinke not. Who was first
Head of that Massacre?

BALIGNY
The Guise.

CLERMONT
Tis nothing so.
Who was in fault for all the slaughters made
In Ilion, and about it? Were the Greekes?
Was it not Paris ravishing the Queene
Of Lacædemon; breach of shame and faith,
And all the lawes of hospitalitie?
This is the beastly slaughter made of men,
When truth is over-throwne, his lawes corrupted;
When soules are smother'd in the flatter'd flesh,
Slaine bodies are no more then oxen slaine.

BALIGNY
Differ not men from oxen?

CLERMONT

Who sayes so?
But see wherein; in the understanding rules
Of their opinions, lives, and actions;
In their communities of faith and reason.
Was not the wolfe that nourisht Romulus
More humane then the men that did expose him?

BALIGNY

That makes against you.

CLERMONT

Not, sir, if you note
That by that deede, the actions difference make
Twixt men and beasts, and not their names nor formes.
Had faith, nor shame, all hospitable rights
Beene broke by Troy, Greece had not made that slaughter.
Had that beene sav'd sayes a philosopher
The Iliads and Odysses had beene lost.
Had Faith and true Religion beene prefer'd
Religious Guise had never massacerd.

BALIGNY

Well, sir, I cannot, when I meete with you,
But thus digresse a little, for my learning,
From any other businesse I entend.
But now the voyage we resolv'd for Cambray,
I told the Guise, beginnes; and wee must haste.
And till the Lord Renel hath found some meane
(Conspiring with the Countesse) to make sure
Your sworne wreake on her husband, though this fail'd,
In my so brave command wee'll spend the time,
Sometimes in training out in skirmishes
And battailes all our troopes and companies;
And sometimes breathe your brave Scotch running horse,
That great Guise gave you, that all th'horse in France
Farre over-runnes at every race and hunting
Both of the hare and deere. You shall be honor'd
Like the great Guise himselfe, above the King.
And (can you but appease your great-spleen'd sister
For our delaid wreake of your brothers slaughter)
At all parts you'll be welcom'd to your wonder.

CLERMONT

Ile see my lord the Guise againe before
Wee take our journey?

BALIGNY

O, sir, by all meanes;

You cannot be too carefull of his love,
That ever takes occasion to be raising
Your virtues past the reaches of this age,
And rankes you with the best of th'ancient Romanes.

CLERMONT
That praise at no part moves mee, but the worth
Of all hee can give others spher'd in him.

BALIGNY
Hee yet is thought to entertaine strange aymes.

CLERMONT
He may be well; yet not, as you thinke, strange.
His strange aymes are to crosse the common custome
Of servile Nobles; in which hee's so ravisht,
That quite the earth he leaves, and up hee leapes
On Atlas shoulders, and from thence lookes downe,
Viewing how farre off other high ones creepe;
Rich, poore of reason, wander; all pale looking,
And trembling but to thinke of their sure deaths,
Their lives so base are, and so rancke their breaths.
Which I teach Guise to heighten, and make sweet
With lifes deare odors, a good minde and name;
For which hee onely loves me, and deserves
My love and life, which through all deaths I vow:
Resolving this (what ever change can be)
Thou hast created, thou hast ruinde mee.

[Exit.

ACTUS TERTII

SCÆNA PRIMA

A Parade-Ground near Cambrai

A march of **CAPTAINES** over the Stage.

MAILLARD, CHALON, AUMALE following with **SOLDIERS**.

MAILLARD
These troopes and companies come in with wings:
So many men, so arm'd, so gallant horse,
I thinke no other government in France
So soone could bring together. With such men

Me thinkes a man might passe th'insulting Pillars
Of Bacchus and Alcides.

CHALON
I much wonder
Our Lord Lieutenant brought his brother downe
To feast and honour him, and yet now leaves him
At such an instance.

MAILLARD
Twas the Kings command;
For whom he must leave brother, wife, friend, all things.

AUMALE
The confines of his government, whose view
Is the pretext of his command, hath neede
Of no such sodaine expedition.

MAILLARD
Wee must not argue that. The Kings command
Is neede and right enough: and that he serves,
(As all true subjects should) without disputing.

CHALON
But knowes not hee of your command to take
His brother Clermont?

MAILLARD
No: the Kings will is
Expressely to conceale his apprehension
From my Lord Governour. Observ'd yee not?
Againe peruse the letters. Both you are
Made my assistants, and have right and trust
In all the waightie secrets like my selfe.

AUMALE
Tis strange a man that had, through his life past,
So sure a foote in vertue and true knowledge
As Clermont D'Ambois, should be now found tripping,
And taken up thus, so to make his fall
More steepe and head-long.

MAILLARD
It is Vertues fortune,
To keepe her low, and in her proper place;
Height hath no roome for her. But as a man
That hath a fruitfull wife, and every yeere
A childe by her, hath every yeere a month

To breathe himselfe, where hee that gets no childe
Hath not a nights rest (if he will doe well);
So, let one marry this same barraine Vertue,
She never lets him rest, where fruitfull Vice
Spares her rich drudge, gives him in labour breath,
Feedes him with bane, and makes him fat with death.

CHALON
I see that good lives never can secure
Men from bad livers. Worst men will have best
As ill as they, or heaven to hell they'll wrest.

AUMALE
There was a merit for this, in the fault
That Bussy made, for which he (doing pennance)
Proves that these foule adulterous guilts will runne
Through the whole bloud, which not the cleare can shunne.

MAILLARD
Ile therefore take heede of the bastarding
Whole innocent races; tis a fearefull thing.
And as I am true batcheler, I sweare,
To touch no woman to the coupling ends
Unlesse it be mine owne wife or my friends;
I may make bold with him.

AUMALE
Tis safe and common.
The more your friend dares trust, the more deceive him.
And as through dewie vapors the sunnes forme
Makes the gay rainebow girdle to a storme,
So in hearts hollow, friendship (even the sunne
To all good growing in societie)
Makes his so glorious and divine name hold
Collours for all the ill that can be told.

[Trumpets within.

MAILLARD
Harke! our last troopes are come.

[Drums beate.

CHALON
Harke! our last foote.

MAILLARD
Come, let us put all quickly into battaile,

And send for Clermont, in whose honour all
This martiall preparation wee pretend.

CHALON
Wee must bethinke us, ere wee apprehend him,
(Besides our maine strength) of some stratageme
To make good our severe command on him,
As well to save blood as to make him sure:
For if hee come on his Scotch horse, all France
Put at the heeles of him will faile to take him.

MAILLARD
What thinke you if wee should disguise a brace
Of our best souldiers in faire lackies coates,
And send them for him, running by his side,
Till they have brought him in some ambuscado
We close may lodge for him, and sodainely
Lay sure hand on him, plucking him from horse?

AUMALE
It must be sure and strong hand; for if once
Hee feeles the touch of such a stratageme,
Tis not choicest brace of all our bands
Can manacle or quench his fiery hands.

MAILLARD
When they have seaz'd him, the ambush shal make in.

AUMALE
Doe as you please; his blamelesse spirit deserves
(I dare engage my life) of all this, nothing.

CHALON
Why should all this stirre be, then?

AUMALE
Who knowes not
The bumbast politie thrusts into his gyant,
To make his wisedome seeme of size as huge,
And all for sleight encounter of a shade,
So hee be toucht, hee would have hainous made?

MAILLARD
It may be once so; but so ever, never.
Ambition is abroad, on foote, on horse;
Faction chokes every corner, streete, the Court;
Whose faction tis you know, and who is held
The fautors right hand: how high his aymes reach

Nought but a crowne can measure. This must fall
Past shadowes waights, and is most capitall.

CHALON
No question; for since hee is come to Cambray,
The malecontent, decaid Marquesse Renel,
Is come, and new arriv'd; and made partaker
Of all the entertaining showes and feasts
That welcom'd Clermont to the brave virago,
His manly sister. Such wee are esteem'd
As are our consorts. Marquesse malecontent
Comes where hee knowes his vaine hath safest vent.

MAILLARD
Let him come at his will, and goe as free;
Let us ply Clermont, our whole charge is hee.

[Exeunt.

SCÆNA SECUNDA

A Room in the Governor's Castle at Cambrai

Enter a **GENTLEMAN USHER** before **CLERMONT: RENEL, CHARLOTTE**, with **TWO WOMEN ATTENDANTS**, with **OTHERS**: showes having past within.

CHARLOTTE
This for your lordships welcome into Cambrai.

RENEL
Noblest of ladies, tis beyond all power
Were my estate at first full in my meanes
To quit or merit.

CLERMONT
You come something latter
From Court, my lord, then I: and since newes there
Is every day encreasing with th'affaires,
Must I not aske now, what the newes is there?
Where the Court lyes? what stirre? change? what avise
From England, Italie?

RENEL
You must doe so,
If you'll be cald a gentleman well quallified,
And weare your time and wits in those discourses.

CLERMONT

The Locrian princes therefore were brave rulers;
For whosoever there came new from countrie,
And in the citie askt, "What newes?" was punisht:
Since commonly such braines are most delighted
With innovations, gossips tales, and mischiefes.
But as of lyons it is said and eagles,
That, when they goe, they draw their seeres and tallons
Close up, to shunne rebating of their sharpnesse:
So our wits sharpnesse, which wee should employ
In noblest knowledge, wee should never waste
In vile and vulgar admirations.

RENEL

Tis right; but who, save onely you, performes it,
And your great brother? Madame, where is he?

CHARLOTTE

Gone, a day since, into the countries confines,
To see their strength, and readinesse for service.

RENEL

Tis well; his favour with the King hath made him
Most worthily great, and live right royally.

CLERMONT

I: would hee would not doe so! Honour never
Should be esteem'd with wise men as the price
And value of their virtuous services,
But as their signe or badge; for that bewrayes
More glory in the outward grace of goodnesse
Then in the good it selfe; and then tis said,
Who more joy takes that men his good advance
Then in the good it selfe, does it by chance.

CHARLOTTE

My brother speakes all principle. What man
Is mov'd with your soule? or hath such a thought
In any rate of goodnesse?

CLERMONT

Tis their fault.
We have examples of it, cleare and many.
Demetrius Phalerius, an orator,
And (which not oft meete) a philosopher,
So great in Athens grew that he erected
Three hundred statues of him; of all which,

No rust nor length of time corrupted one;
But in his life time all were overthrowne.
And Demades (that past Demosthenes
For all extemporall orations)
Erected many statues, which (he living)
Were broke, and melted into chamber-pots.
Many such ends have fallen on such proud honours,
No more because the men on whom they fell
Grew insolent and left their vertues state,
Then for their hugenesse, that procur'd their hate:
And therefore little pompe in men most great
Makes mightily and strongly to the guard
Of what they winne by chance or just reward.
Great and immodest braveries againe,
Like statues much too high made for their bases,
Are overturn'd as soone as given their places.

[Enter a **MESSENGER** with a Letter.

MESSENGER
Here is a letter, sir, deliver'd mee
Now at the fore-gate by a gentleman.

CLERMONT
What gentleman?

MESSENGER
Hee would not tell his name;
Hee said, hee had not time enough to tell it,
And say the little rest hee had to say.

CLERMONT
That was a merry saying; he tooke measure
Of his deare time like a most thriftie husband.

CHARLOTTE
What newes?

CLERMONT
Strange ones, and fit for a novation;
Waightie, unheard of, mischievous enough.

RENEL
Heaven shield! what are they?

CLERMONT
Read them, good my lord.

RENEL

"You are betraid into this countrie." Monstrous!

CHARLOTTE

How's that?

CLERMONT

Read on.

RENEL

"Maillard, your brothers Lieutenant, that yesterday invited you to see his musters, hath letters and strickt charge from the King to apprehend you."

CHARLOTTE

To apprehend him!

RENEL

"Your brother absents himselfe of purpose."

CLERMONT

That's a sound one.

CHARLOTTE

That's a lye.

RENEL

"Get on your Scotch horse, and retire to your strength; you know where it is, and there it expects you. Beleeve this as your best friend had sworne it. Fare-well if you will. Anonymos." What's that?

CLERMONT

Without a name.

CHARLOTTE

And all his notice, too, without all truth.

CLERMONT

So I conceive it, sister: ile not wrong
My well knowne brother for Anonymos.

CHARLOTTE

Some foole hath put this tricke on you, yet more
T'uncover your defect of spirit and valour,
First showne in lingring my deare brothers wreake.
See what it is to give the envious world
Advantage to diminish eminent virtue.
Send him a challenge. Take a noble course
To wreake a murther, done so like a villaine.

CLERMONT
Shall we revenge a villanie with villanie.

CHARLOTTE
Is it not equall?

CLERMONT
Shall wee equall be with villaines?
Is that your reason?

CHARLOTTE
Cowardise evermore
Flyes to the shield of reason.

CLERMONT
Nought that is
Approv'd by reason can be cowardise.

CHARLOTTE
Dispute, when you should fight! Wrong, wreaklesse sleeping,
Makes men dye honorlesse; one borne, another
Leapes on our shoulders.

CLERMONT
Wee must wreake our wrongs
So as wee take not more.

CHARLOTTE
One wreakt in time
Prevents all other. Then shines vertue most
When time is found for facts; and found, not lost.

CLERMONT
No time occurres to Kings, much lesse to vertue;
Nor can we call it vertue that proceedes
From vicious fury. I repent that ever
(By any instigation in th'appearance
My brothers spirit made, as I imagin'd)
That e'er I yeelded to revenge his murther.
All worthy men should ever bring their bloud
To beare all ill, not to be wreakt with good.
Doe ill for no ill; never private cause
Should take on it the part of publike lawes.

CHARLOTTE
A D'Ambois beare in wrong so tame a spirit!

RENEL

Madame, be sure there will be time enough
For all the vengeance your great spirit can wish.
The course yet taken is allow'd by all,
Which being noble, and refus'd by th'Earle,
Now makes him worthy of your worst advantage:
And I have cast a project with the Countesse
To watch a time when all his wariest guards
Shall not exempt him. Therefore give him breath;
Sure death delaid is a redoubled death.

CLERMONT
Good sister, trouble not your selfe with this:
Take other ladyes care; practise your face.
There's the chaste matron, Madame Perigot,
Dwels not farre hence; Ile ride and send her to you.
Shee did live by retailing mayden-heads
In her minoritie; but now shee deales
In whole-sale altogether for the Court.
I tell you, shee's the onely fashion-monger,
For your complexion, poudring of your haire,
Shadowes, rebatoes, wires, tyres, and such trickes,
That Cambray or, I thinke, the Court affords.
She shall attend you, sister, and with these
Womanly practises emply your spirit;
This other suites you not, nor fits the fashion.
Though shee be deare, lay't on, spare for no cost;
Ladies in these have all their bounties lost.

RENEL
Madame, you see, his spirit will not checke
At any single danger, when it stands
Thus merrily firme against an host of men,
Threaten'd to be in armes for his surprise.

CHARLOTTE
That's a meere bugge-beare, an impossible mocke.
If hee, and him I bound by nuptiall faith,
Had not beene dull and drossie in performing
Wreake of the deare bloud of my matchlesse brother,
What Prince, what King, which of the desperat'st ruffings,
Outlawes in Arden, durst have tempted thus
One of our bloud and name, be't true or false?

CLERMONT
This is not caus'd by that; twill be as sure
As yet it is not, though this should be true.

CHARLOTTE

True, tis past thought false.

CLERMONT
I suppose the worst,
Which farre I am from thinking; and despise
The armie now in battaile that should act it.

CHARLOTTE
I would not let my bloud up to that thought,
But it should cost the dearest bloud in France.

CLERMONT
Sweet sister, farre be both off as the fact
Of my fain'd apprehension.

CHARLOTTE
I would once
Strip off my shame with my attire, and trie
If a poore woman, votist of revenge,
Would not performe it with a president
To all you bungling, foggy-spirited men.
But for our birth-rights honour, doe not mention
One syllable of any word may goe
To the begetting of an act so tender
And full of sulphure as this letters truth:
It comprehends so blacke a circumstance
Not to be nam'd, that but to forme one thought,
It is or can be so, would make me mad.
Come, my lord, you and I will fight this dreame
Out at the chesse.

RENEL
Most gladly, worthiest ladie.

[Exeunt **CHARLOTTE** and **RENEL**.

[Enter a **MESSENGER**.

MESSENGER.
Sir, my Lord Governours Lieutenant prayes
Accesse to you.

CLERMONT
Himselfe alone?

MESSENGER
Alone, sir.

CLERMONT
Attend him in.

[Exit **MESSENGER**.

Now comes this plot to tryall;
I shall descerne (if it be true as rare)
Some sparkes will flye from his dissembling eyes.
Ile sound his depth.

[Enter **MAILLARD** with the **MESSENGER**.

MAILLARD
Honour, and all things noble!

CLERMONT
As much to you, good Captaine. What's th'affaire?

MAILLARD
Sir, the poore honour we can adde to all
Your studyed welcome to this martiall place,
In presentation of what strength consists
My lord your brothers government, is readie.
I have made all his troopes and companies
Advance and put themselves in battailia,
That you may see both how well arm'd they are
How strong is every troope and companie,
How ready, and how well prepar'd for service.

CLERMONT
And must they take mee?

MAILLARD
Take you, sir! O heaven!

MESSENGER [aside, to **CLERMONT**]
Beleeve it, sir, his count'nance
chang'd in turning.

MAILLARD
What doe you meane, sir?

CLERMONT
If you have charg'd them,
You being charg'd your selfe, to apprehend mee,
Turne not your face; throw not your lookes about so.

MAILLARD

Pardon me, sir. You amaze me to conceive
From whence our wils to honour you should turne
To such dishonour of my lord, your brother.
Dare I, without him, undertake your taking?

CLERMONT
Why not? by your direct charge from the King.

MAILLARD
By my charge from the King! would he so much
Disgrace my lord, his owne Lieutenant here,
To give me his command without his forfaite?

CLERMONT
Acts that are done by Kings, are not askt why.
Ile not dispute the case, but I will search you.

MAILLARD
Search mee! for what?

CLERMONT
For letters.

MAILLARD
I beseech you,
Doe not admit one thought of such a shame
To a commander.

CLERMONT
Goe to! I must doo't.
Stand and be searcht; you know mee.

MAILLARD
You forget
What tis to be a captaine, and your selfe.

CLERMONT
Stand, or I vow to heaven, Ile make you lie,
Never to rise more.

MAILLARD
If a man be mad,
Reason must beare him.

CLERMONT
So coy to be searcht?

MAILLARD

Sdeath, sir, use a captaine like a carrier!

CLERMONT
Come, be not furious; when I have done,
You shall make such a carrier of me,
If't be your pleasure: you're my friend, I know,
And so am bold with you.

MAILLARD
You'll nothing finde
Where nothing is.

CLERMONT
Sweare you have nothing.

MAILLARD
Nothing you seeke, I sweare. I beseech you,
Know I desir'd this out of great affection,
To th'end my lord may know out of your witnesse
His forces are not in so bad estate
As hee esteem'd them lately in your hearing;
For which he would not trust me with the confines,
But went himselfe to witnesse their estate.

CLERMONT
I heard him make that reason, and am sorie
I had no thought of it before I made
Thus bold with you, since tis such ruberb to you.
Ile therefore search no more. If you are charg'd
(By letters from the King, or otherwise)
To apprehend me, never spice it more
With forc'd tearmes of your love, but say: I yeeld;
Holde, take my sword, here; I forgive thee freely;
Take; doe thine office.

MAILLARD
Sfoote! you make m'a hang-man;
By all my faith to you, there's no such thing.

CLERMONT
Your faith to mee!

MAILLARD
My faith to God; all's one:
Who hath no faith to men, to God hath none.

CLERMONT
In that sense I accept your othe, and thanke you.

I gave my word to goe, and I will goe.

[Exit **CLERMONT**.

MAILLARD
Ile watch you whither.

[Exit **MAILLARD**.

MESSENGER
If hee goes, hee proves
How vaine are mens fore knowledges of things,
When heaven strikes blinde their powers of note and use,
And makes their way to ruine seeme more right
Then that which safetie opens to their sight.
Cassandra's prophecie had no more profit
With Troyes blinde citizens, when shee foretolde
Troyes ruine; which, succeeding, made her use
This "sacred" inclamation: "God" (said shee)
"Would have me utter things uncredited;
For which now they approve what I presag'd;
They count me wise, that said before, I rag'd."

[Exit.

SCÆNA TERTIA

A Camp near Cambrai

Enter **CHALON** with two **SOLDIERS**.

CHALON
Come, souldiers: you are downewards fit for lackies;
Give me your pieces, and take you these coates,
To make you compleate foot men, in whose formes
You must be compleate souldiers: you two onely
Stand for our armie.

1st SOLDIER
That were much.

CHALON
Tis true;
You two must doe, or enter, what our armie
Is now in field for.

2nd SOLDIER
I see then our guerdon
Must be the deede it selfe, twill be such honour.

CHALON
What fight souldiers most for?

1st SOLDIER
Honour onely.

CHALON
Yet here are crownes beside.

1st SOLDIER
We thanke you, Captaine.

2nd SOLDIER
Now, sir, how show wee?

CHALON
As you should at all parts.
Goe now to Clermont D'Ambois, and informe him,
Two battailes are set ready in his honour,
And stay his presence onely for their signall,
When they shall joyne; and that, t'attend him hither
Like one wee so much honour, wee have sent him—

1st SOLDIER
Us two in person.

CHALON
Well, sir, say it so;
And having brought him to the field, when I
Fall in with him, saluting, get you both
Of one side of his horse, and plucke him downe,
And I with th'ambush laid will second you.

1st SOLDIER
Nay, we shall lay on hands of too much strength
To neede your secondings.

2nd SOLDIER
I hope we shall.
Two are enough to encounter Hercules.

CHALON
Tis well said, worthy souldiers; hast, and hast him.

[Exeunt.

SCÆNA QUARTA

A Room in the Governor's Castle at Cambrai

Enter **CLERMONT, MAILLARD** close following him.

CLERMONT
My Scotch horse to their armie—

MAILLARD
Please you, sir?

CLERMONT
Sdeath! you're passing diligent.

MAILLARD
Of my soule,
Tis onely in my love to honour you
With what would grace the King: but since I see
You still sustaine a jealous eye on mee,
Ile goe before.

CLERMONT
Tis well; Ile come; my hand.

MAILLARD
Your hand, sir! Come, your word; your choise be us'd.

[Exit.

[**CLERMONT** solus.

CLERMONT
I had an aversation to this voyage,
When first my brother mov'd it, and have found
That native power in me was never vaine;
Yet now neglected it. I wonder much
At my inconstancie in these decrees
I every houre set downe to guide my life.
When Homer made Achilles passionate,
Wrathfull, revengefull, and insatiate
In his affections, what man will denie
He did compose it all of industrie
To let men see that men of most renowne,

Strong'st, noblest, fairest, if they set not downe
Decrees within them, for disposing these,
Of judgement, resolution, uprightnesse,
And certaine knowledge of their use and ends,
Mishap and miserie no lesse extends
To their destruction, with all that they pris'd,
Then to the poorest and the most despis'd?

[Enter **RENEL**.

RENEL
Why, how now, friend, retir'd! take heede you prove not
Dismaid with this strange fortune. All observe you:
Your government's as much markt as the Kings.
What said a friend to Pompey?

CLERMONT
What?

RENEL
The people
Will never know, unlesse in death thou trie,
That thou know'st how to beare adversitie.

CLERMONT
I shall approve how vile I value feare
Of death at all times; but to be too rash,
Without both will and care to shunne the worst,
(It being in power to doe well and with cheere)
Is stupid negligence and worse then feare.

RENEL
Suppose this true now.

CLERMONT
No, I cannot doo't.
My sister truely said, there hung a taile
Of circumstance so blacke on that supposure,
That to sustaine it thus abhorr'd our mettall.
And I can shunne it too, in spight of all,
Not going to field; and there to, being so mounted
As I will, since I goe.

RENEL
You will then goe?

CLERMONT
I am engag'd both in my word and hand.

But this is it that makes me thus retir'd,
To call my selfe t'account, how this affaire
Is to be manag'd, if the worst should chance:
With which I note, how dangerous it is
For any man to prease beyond the place
To which his birth, or meanes, or knowledge ties him.
For my part, though of noble birth, my birthright
Had little left it, and I know tis better
To live with little, and to keepe within
A mans owne strength still, and in mans true end,
Then runne a mixt course. Good and bad hold never
Any thing common; you can never finde
Things outward care, but you neglect your minde.
God hath the whole world perfect made and free;
His parts to th'use of th'All. Men, then, that are
Parts of that All, must, as the generall sway
Of that importeth, willingly obay
In every thing without their power to change.
Hee that, unpleas'd to hold his place, will range,
Can in no other be contain'd that's fit,
And so resisting th'All is crusht with it:
But he that knowing how divine a frame
The whole world is, and of it all can name
(Without selfe-flatterie) no part so divine
As hee himselfe; and therefore will confine
Freely his whole powers in his proper part,
Goes on most God-like. Hee that strives t'invert
The Universals course with his poore way,
Not onely dust-like shivers with the sway,
But crossing God in his great worke, all earth
Beares not so cursed and so damn'd a birth.

RENEL
Goe on; Ile take no care what comes of you;
Heaven will not see it ill, how ere it show.
But the pretext to see these battailes rang'd
Is much your honour.

CLERMONT
As the world esteemes it.
But to decide that, you make me remember
An accident of high and noble note,
And fits the subject of my late discourse
Of holding on our free and proper way.
I over-tooke, comming from Italie,
In Germanie a great and famous Earle
Of England, the most goodly fashion'd man
I ever saw; from head to foote in forme

Rare and most absolute; hee had a face
Like one of the most ancient honour'd Romanes
From whence his noblest familie was deriv'd;
He was beside of spirit passing great,
Valiant, and learn'd, and liberall as the sunne,
Spoke and writ sweetly, or of learned subjects,
Or of the discipline of publike weales;
And t'was the Earle of Oxford: and being offer'd
At that time, by Duke Cassimere, the view
Of his right royall armie then in field,
Refus'd it, and no foote was mov'd to stirre
Out of his owne free fore-determin'd course.
I, wondring at it, askt for it his reason,
It being an offer so much for his honour.
Hee, all acknowledging, said t'was not fit
To take those honours that one cannot quit.

RENEL
Twas answer'd like the man you have describ'd.

CLERMONT
And yet he cast it onely in the way,
To stay and serve the world. Nor did it fit
His owne true estimate how much it waigh'd;
For hee despis'd it, and esteem'd it freer
To keepe his owne way straight, and swore that hee
Had rather make away his whole estate
In things that crost the vulgar then he would
Be frozen up stiffe (like a Sir John Smith,
His countrey-man) in common Nobles fashions;
Affecting, as't the end of noblesse were,
Those servile observations.

RENEL
It was strange.

CLERMONT
O tis a vexing sight to see a man,
Out of his way, stalke proud as hee were in;
Out of his way, to be officious,
Observant, wary, serious, and grave,
Fearefull, and passionate, insulting, raging,
Labour with iron flailes to thresh downe feathers
Flitting in ayre.

RENEL
What one considers this,
Of all that are thus out? or once endevours,

Erring, to enter on mans right-hand path?

CLERMONT
These are too grave for brave wits; give them toyes;
Labour bestow'd on these is harsh and thriftlesse.
If you would Consull be (sayes one) of Rome,
You must be watching, starting out of sleepes;
Every way whisking; gloryfying Plebeians;
Kissing Patricians hands, rot at their dores;
Speake and doe basely; every day bestow
Gifts and observance upon one or other:
And what's th'event of all? Twelve rods before thee;
Three or foure times sit for the whole tribunall;
Exhibite Circean games; make publike feasts;
And for these idle outward things (sayes he)
Would'st thou lay on such cost, toile, spend thy spirits?
And to be voide of perturbation,
For constancie, sleepe when thou would'st have sleepe,
Wake when thou would'st wake, feare nought, vexe for nought,
No paines wilt thou bestow? no cost? no thought?

RENEL
What should I say? As good consort with you
As with an angell; I could heare you ever.

CLERMONT
Well, in, my lord, and spend time with my sister,
And keepe her from the field with all endeavour.
The souldiers love her so, and shee so madly
Would take my apprehension, if it chance,
That bloud would flow in rivers.

RENEL
Heaven forbid!
And all with honour your arrivall speede!

[Exit.

[Enter **MESSENGER** with **TWO SOLDIERS** like Lackies.

MESSENGER
Here are two lackies, sir, have message to you.

CLERMONT
What is your message? and from whom, my friends?

1st SOLDIER
From the Lieutenant, Colonell, and the Captaines,

Who sent us to informe you that the battailes
Stand ready rang'd, expecting but your presence
To be their honor'd signall when to joyne,
And we are charg'd to runne by, and attend you.

CLERMONT
I come. I pray you see my running horse
Brought to the backe-gate to mee.

MESSENGER
Instantly.

[Exit **MESSENGER**.

CLERMONT
Chance what can chance mee, well or ill is equall
In my acceptance, since I joy in neyther,
But goe with sway of all the world together.
In all successes Fortune and the day
To mee alike are; I am fixt, be shee
Never so fickle; and will there repose,
Farre past the reach of any dye she throwes.

[Exit.

ACTUS QUARTI

SCÆNA PRIMA

A Parade-Ground near Cambrai

Alarum within: Excursions over the Stage.

The **SOLDIERS** disguised as Lackies running, **MAILLARD** following them.

MAILLARD
Villaines, not hold him when ye had him downe!

1st SOLDIER
Who can hold lightning? Sdeath a man as well
Might catch a canon bullet in his mouth,
And spit it in your hands, as take and hold him.

MAILLARD
Pursue, enclose him! stand or fall on him,
And yee may take him. Sdeath! they make him guards.

[Exit.

Alarum still, and enter **CHALON**.

CHALON
Stand, cowards, stand; strike, send your bullets at him.

1st SOLDIER
Wee came to entertaine him, sir, for honour.

2nd SOLDIER
Did ye not say so?

CHALON
Slaves, hee is a traitor;
Command the horse troopes to over-runne the traitor.

[Exeunt.

Shouts within. Alarum still, and Chambers shot off. Then enter **AUMALE**.

AUMALE
What spirit breathes thus in this more then man,
Turnes flesh to ayre possest, and in a storme
Teares men about the field like autumne leaves?
He turnd wilde lightning in the lackies hands,
Who, though their sodaine violent twitch unhorst him,
Yet when he bore himselfe, their saucie fingers
Flew as too hot off, as hee had beene fire.
The ambush then made in, through all whose force
Hee drave as if a fierce and fire-given canon
Had spit his iron vomit out amongst them.
The battailes then in two halfe-moones enclos'd him,
In which he shew'd as if he were the light,
And they but earth, who, wondring what hee was,
Shruncke their steele hornes and gave him glorious passe.
And as a great shot from a towne besieg'd
At foes before it flyes forth blacke and roring,
But they too farre, and that with waight opprest
(As if disdaining earth) doth onely grasse,
Strike earth, and up againe into the ayre,
Againe sinkes to it, and againe doth rise,
And keepes such strength that when it softliest moves
It piece-meale shivers any let it proves—
So flew brave Clermont forth, till breath forsooke him,
Then fell to earth; and yet (sweet man) even then
His spirits convulsions made him bound againe

Past all their reaches; till, all motion spent,
His fixt eyes cast a blaze of such disdaine,
All stood and star'd, and untouch'd let him lie,
As something sacred fallen out of the skie.

[A cry within.

O now some rude hand hath laid hold on him!

[Enter **MAILLARD, CHALON** leading **CLERMONT, CAPTAINES** and **SOLDIERS** following.

See, prisoner led, with his bands honour'd more
Then all the freedome he enjoy'd before.

MAILLARD
At length wee have you, sir.

CLERMONT
You have much joy too;
I made you sport. Yet, but I pray you tell mee,
Are not you perjur'd?

MAILLARD
No: I swore for the King.

CLERMONT
Yet perjurie, I hope, is perjurie.

MAILLARD
But thus forswearing is not perjurie.
You are no politician: not a fault,
How foule soever, done for private ends,
Is fault in us sworne to the publike good:
Wee never can be of the damned crew;
Wee may impolitique our selves (as 'twere)
Into the kingdomes body politique,
Whereof indeede we're members; you misse termes.

CLERMONT
The things are yet the same.

MAILLARD
Tis nothing so; the propertie is alter'd:
Y'are no lawyer. Or say that othe and othe
Are still the same in number, yet their species
Differ extreamely, as, for flat example,
When politique widowes trye men for their turne,
Before they wed them, they are harlots then,

But when they wed them, they are honest women:
So private men, when they forsweare, betray,
Are perjur'd treachers, but being publique once,
That is, sworne-married to the publique good—

CLERMONT
Are married women publique?

MAILLARD
Publique good;
For marriage makes them, being the publique good,
And could not be without them: so I say
Men publique, that is, being sworne-married
To the good publique, being one body made
With the realmes body politique, are no more
Private, nor can be perjur'd, though forsworne,
More then a widow married, for the act
Of generation is for that an harlot,
Because for that shee was so, being unmarried:
An argument a paribus.

CHALON
Tis a shrow'd one.

CLERMONT
"Who hath no faith to men, to God hath none:"
Retaine you that, sir? who said so?

MAILLARD
Twas I.

CLERMONT
Thy owne tongue damne thy infidelitie!
But, Captaines all, you know me nobly borne;
Use yee t'assault such men as I with lackyes?

CHALON
They are no lackyes, sir, but souldiers
Disguis'd in lackyes coates.

1st SOLDIER
Sir, wee have seene the enemie.

CLERMONT
Avant! yee rascols, hence!

MAILLARD
Now leave your coates.

CLERMONT

Let me not see them more.

AUMALE

I grieve that vertue lives so undistinguisht
From vice in any ill, and though the crowne
Of soveraigne law, shee should be yet her footstoole,
Subject to censure, all the shame and paine
Of all her rigor.

CLERMONT

Yet false policie
Would cover all, being like offenders hid,
That (after notice taken where they hide)
The more they crouch and stirre, the more are spide.

AUMALE

I wonder how this chanc'd you.

CLERMONT

Some informer,
Bloud-hound to mischiefe, usher to the hang-man,
Thirstie of honour for some huge state act,
Perceiving me great with the worthy Guise,
And he (I know not why) held dangerous,
Made me the desperate organe of his danger,
Onely with that poore colour: tis the common
And more then whore-like tricke of treacherie
And vermine bred to rapine and to ruine,
For which this fault is still to be accus'd;
Since good acts faile, crafts and deceits are us'd.
If it be other, never pittie mee.

AUMALE

Sir, we are glad, beleeve it, and have hope
The King will so conceit it.

CLERMONT

At his pleasure.
In meane time, what's your will, Lord Lieutenant?

MAILLARD

To leave your owne horse, and to mount the trumpets.

CLERMONT

It shall be done. This heavily prevents
My purpos'd recreation in these parts;

Which now I thinke on, let mee begge you, sir,
To lend me some one captaine of your troopes,
To beare the message of my haplesse service
And miserie to my most noble mistresse,
Countesse of Cambray; to whose house this night
I promist my repaire, and know most truely,
With all the ceremonies of her favour,
She sure expects mee.

MAILLARD
Thinke you now on that?

CLERMONT
On that, sir? I, and that so worthily,
That if the King, in spight of your great service,
Would send me instant promise of enlargement,
Condition I would set this message by,
I would not take it, but had rather die.

AUMALE
Your message shall be done, sir: I, my selfe,
Will be for you a messenger of ill.

CLERMONT
I thanke you, sir, and doubt not yet to live
To quite your kindnesse.

AUMALE
Meane space use your spirit
And knowledge for the chearfull patience
Of this so strange and sodaine consequence.

CLERMONT
Good sir, beleeve that no particular torture
Can force me from my glad obedience
To any thing the high and generall Cause,
To match with his whole fabricke, hath ordainde;
And know yee all (though farre from all your aymes,
Yet worth them all, and all mens endlesse studies)
That in this one thing, all the discipline
Of manners and of manhood is contain'd:—
A man to joyne himselfe with th'Universe
In his maine sway, and make (in all things fit)
One with that all, and goe on round as it;
Not plucking from the whole his wretched part,
And into straites, or into nought revert,
Wishing the compleate Universe might be
Subject to such a ragge of it as hee;

But to consider great Necessitie
All things, as well refract as voluntarie,
Reduceth to the prime celestiall cause;
Which he that yeelds to with a mans applause,
And cheeke by cheeke goes, crossing it no breath,
But like Gods image followes to the death,
That man is truely wise, and every thing
(Each cause and every part distinguishing)
In nature with enough art understands,
And that full glory merits at all hands
That doth the whole world at all parts adorne,
And appertaines to one celestiall borne.

[Exeunt **OMNES**.

SCÆNA SECUNDA

A Room at the Court in Paris

Enter **BALIGNY, RENEL.**

BALIGNY
So foule a scandall never man sustain'd,
Which caus'd by th'King is rude and tyrannous:
Give me a place, and my Lieutenant make
The filler of it!

RENEL
I should never looke
For better of him; never trust a man
For any justice, that is rapt with pleasure;
To order armes well, that makes smockes his ensignes,
And his whole governments sayles: you heard of late
Hee had the foure and twenty wayes of venerie
Done all before him.

BALIGNY
Twas abhorr'd and beastly.

RENEL
Tis more then natures mightie hand can doe
To make one humane and a letcher too.
Looke how a wolfe doth like a dogge appeare,
So like a friend is an adulterer;
Voluptuaries, and these belly-gods,
No more true men are then so many toads.

A good man happy is a common good;
Vile men advanc'd live of the common bloud.

BALIGNY

Give, and then take, like children!

RENEL

Bounties are
As soone repented as they happen rare.

BALIGNY

What should Kings doe, and men of eminent places,
But, as they gather, sow gifts to the graces?
And where they have given, rather give againe
(Being given for vertue) then, like babes and fooles,
Take and repent gifts? why are wealth and power?

RENEL

Power and wealth move to tyranny, not bountie;
The merchant for his wealth is swolne in minde,
When yet the chiefe lord of it is the winde.

BALIGNY

That may so chance to our state-merchants too;
Something performed, that hath not farre to goe.

RENEL

That's the maine point, my lord; insist on that.

BALIGNY

But doth this fire rage further? hath it taken
The tender tynder of my wifes sere bloud?
Is shee so passionate?

RENEL

So wilde, so mad,
Shee cannot live and this unwreakt sustaine.
The woes are bloudy that in women raigne.
The Sicile gulfe keepes feare in lesse degree;
There is no tyger not more tame then shee.

BALIGNY

There is no looking home, then?

RENEL

Home! Medea
With all her hearbs, charmes, thunders, lightning,
Made not her presence and blacke hants more dreadfull.

BALIGNY
Come, to the King; if he reforme not all,
Marke the event, none stand where that must fall.

[Exeunt.

SCÆNA TERTIA

A Room in the House of the Countess of Cambrai

Enter **COUNTESS, RIOVA,** and an **USHER.**

USHER
Madame, a captaine come from Clermont D'Ambois
Desires accesse to you.

COUNTESS
And not himselfe?

USHER
No, madame.

COUNTESS
That's not well. Attend him in.

[Exit **USHER.**

The last houre of his promise now runne out!
And hee breake, some brack's in the frame of nature
That forceth his breach.

[Enter **USHER** and **AUMALE.**

AUMALE
Save your ladiship!

COUNTESS
All welcome! Come you from my worthy servant?

AUMALE
I, madame, and conferre such newes from him—

COUNTESS
Such newes! what newes?

AUMALE

Newes that I wish some other had the charge of.

COUNTESS

O, what charge? what newes?

AUMALE

Your ladiship must use some patience,
Or else I cannot doe him that desire
He urg'd with such affection to your graces.

COUNTESS

Doe it, for heavens love, doe it! if you serve
His kinde desires, I will have patience.
Is hee in health?

AUMALE

He is.

COUNTESS

Why, that's the ground
Of all the good estate wee hold in earth;
All our ill built upon that is no more
Then wee may beare, and should; expresse it all.

AUMALE

Madame, tis onely this; his libertie—

COUNTESS

His libertie! Without that health is nothing.
Why live I, but to aske in doubt of that?
Is that bereft him?

AUMALE

You'll againe prevent me.

COUNTESS

No more, I sweare; I must heare, and together
Come all my miserie! Ile hold, though I burst.

AUMALE

Then, madame, thus it fares; he was envited,
By way of honour to him, to take view
Of all the powers his brother Baligny
Hath in his government; which rang'd in battailes,
Maillard, Lieutenant to the Governour,
Having receiv'd strickt letters from the King,
To traine him to the musters and betray him

To their supprise; which, with Chalon in chiefe,
And other captaines (all the field put hard
By his incredible valour for his scape)
They haplesly and guiltlesly perform'd;
And to Bastile hee's now led prisoner.

COUNTESS
What change is here! how are my hopes prevented!
O my most faithfull servant, thou betraid!
Will Kings make treason lawfull? Is societie
(To keepe which onely Kings were first ordain'd)
Lesse broke in breaking faith twixt friend and friend
Then twixt the King and subject? let them feare
Kings presidents in licence lacke no danger.
Kings are compar'd to Gods, and should be like them,
Full in all right, in nought superfluous,
Nor nothing straining past right for their right.
Raigne justly, and raigne safely. Policie
Is but a guard corrupted, and a way
Venter'd in desarts, without guide or path.
Kings punish subjects errors with their owne.
Kings are like archers, and their subjects, shafts:
For as when archers let their arrowes flye,
They call to them, and bid them flye or fall,
As if twere in the free power of the shaft
To flye or fall, when onely tis the strength,
Straight shooting, compasse given it by the archer,
That makes it hit or misse; and doing eyther,
Hee's to be prais'd or blam'd, and not the shaft:
So Kings to subjects crying, "Doe, doe not this,"
Must to them by their owne examples strength,
The straightnesse of their acts, and equall compasse,
Give subjects power t'obey them in the like;
Not shoote them forth with faultie ayme and strength,
And lay the fault in them for flying amisse.

AUMALE
But for your servant, I dare sweare him guiltlesse.

COUNTESS
Hee would not for his kingdome traitor be;
His lawes are not so true to him, as he.
O knew I how to free him, by way forc'd
Through all their armie, I would flye, and doe it:
And had I of my courage and resolve
But tenne such more, they should not all retaine him.
But I will never die, before I give
Maillard an hundred slashes with a sword,

Chalon an hundred breaches with a pistoll.
They could not all have taken Clermont D'Ambois
Without their treacherie; he had bought his bands out
With their slave blouds: but he was credulous;
Hee would beleeve, since he would be beleev'd;
Your noblest natures are most credulous.
Who gives no trust, all trust is apt to breake;
Hate like hell mouth who thinke not what they speake.

AUMALE
Well, madame, I must tender my attendance
On him againe. Will't please you to returne
No service to him by me?

COUNTESS
Fetch me straight
My little cabinet.

[Exit **ANCILLA**.

Tis little, tell him,
And much too little for his matchlesse love:
But as in him the worths of many men
Are close contracted,—

[Enter **ANCILLA**

—so in this are jewels
Worth many cabinets. Here, with this good sir
Commend my kindest service to my servant,
Thanke him, with all my comforts, and, in them,
With all my life for them; all sent from him
In his remembrance of mee and true love.
And looke you tell him, tell him how I lye
She kneeles downe at his feete.
Prostrate at feet of his accurst misfortune,
Pouring my teares out, which shall ever fall,
Till I have pour'd for him out eyes and all.

AUMALE
O madame, this will kill him; comfort you
With full assurance of his quicke acquitall;
Be not so passionate; rise, cease your teares.

COUNTESS
Then must my life cease. Teares are all the vent
My life hath to scape death. Teares please me better
Then all lifes comforts, being the naturall seede

Of heartie sorrow. As a tree fruit beares,
So doth an undissembled sorrow, teares.

[Hee raises her, and leades her out. Exeunt.

USHER
This might have beene before, and sav'd much charge.

[Exit.

SCÆNA QUARTA

A Room at the Court in Paris

Enter **HENRY, GUISE, BALIGNY, ESPERONE, SOISSONE. PERICOT** with pen, incke, and paper.

GUISE
Now, sir, I hope you're much abus'd eyes see
In my word for my Clermont, what a villaine
Hee was that whisper'd in your jealous eare
His owne blacke treason in suggesting Clermonts,
Colour'd with nothing but being great with mee.
Signe then this writ for his deliverie;
Your hand was never urg'd with worthier boldnesse:
Come, pray, sir, signe it. Why should Kings be praid
To acts of justice? tis a reverence
Makes them despis'd, and showes they sticke and tyre
In what their free powers should be hot as fire.

HENRY
Well, take your will, sir;—Ile have mine ere long.—

[Turns away.

But wherein is this Clermont such a rare one?

GUISE
In his most gentle and unwearied minde,
Rightly to vertue fram'd in very nature;
In his most firme inexorable spirit
To be remov'd from any thing hee chuseth
For worthinesse; or beare the lest perswasion
To what is base, or fitteth not his object;
In his contempt of riches, and of greatnesse
In estimation of th'idolatrous vulgar;
His scorne of all things servile and ignoble,

Though they could gaine him never such advancement;
His liberall kinde of speaking what is truth,
In spight of temporising; the great rising
And learning of his soule so much the more
Against ill fortune, as shee set her selfe
Sharpe against him or would present most hard,
To shunne the malice of her deadliest charge;
His detestation of his speciall friends,
When he perceiv'd their tyrannous will to doe,
Or their abjection basely to sustaine
Any injustice that they could revenge;
The flexibilitie of his most anger,
Even in the maine careere and fury of it,
When any object of desertfull pittie
Offers it selfe to him; his sweet disposure,
As much abhorring to behold as doe
Any unnaturall and bloudy action;
His just contempt of jesters, parasites,
Servile observers, and polluted tongues—
In short, this Senecall man is found in him,
Hee may with heavens immortall powers compare,
To whom the day and fortune equall are;
Come faire or foule, whatever chance can fall,
Fixt in himselfe, hee still is one to all.

HENRY
Showes he to others thus?

OMNES
To all that know him.

HENRY
And apprehend I this man for a traitor?

GUISE
These are your Machevilian villaines,
Your bastard Teucers, that, their mischiefes done,
Runne to your shield for shelter; Cacusses
That cut their too large murtherous theveries
To their dens length still. Woe be to that state
Where treacherie guards, and ruine makes men great!

HENRY
Goe, take my letters for him, and release him.

OMNES
Thankes to your Highnesse; ever live your Highnesse!

[Exeunt.

BALIGNY
Better a man were buried quicke then live
A propertie for state and spoile to thrive.

[Exit.

SCÆNA QUINTA

A Country Road, between Cambrai and Paris

Enter **CLERMONT, MAILLARD, CHALON** with **SOLDIERS**.

MAILLARD
Wee joy you take a chance so ill, so well.

CLERMONT
Who ever saw me differ in acceptance
Of eyther fortune?

CHALON
What, love bad like good!
How should one learne that?

CLERMONT
To love nothing outward,
Or not within our owne powers to command;
And so being sure of every thing we love,
Who cares to lose the rest? if any man
Would neyther live nor dye in his free choise,
But as hee sees necessitie will have it
(Which if hee would resist, he strives in vaine)
What can come neere him that hee doth not well?
And if in worst events his will be done,
How can the best be better? all is one.

MAILLARD
Me thinkes tis prettie.

CLERMONT
Put no difference
If you have this, or not this; but as children
Playing at coites ever regard their game,
And care not for their coites, so let a man
The things themselves that touch him not esteeme,

But his free power in well disposing them.

CHALON
Prettie, from toyes!

CLERMONT
Me thinkes this double disticke
Seemes prettily too to stay superfluous longings:
"Not to have want, what riches doth exceede?
Not to be subject, what superiour thing?
He that to nought aspires, doth nothing neede;
Who breakes no law is subject to no King."

MAILLARD
This goes to mine eare well, I promise you.

CHALON
O, but tis passing hard to stay one thus.

CLERMONT
Tis so; rancke custome raps men so beyond it.
And as tis hard so well mens dores to barre
To keepe the cat out and th'adulterer:
So tis as hard to curbe affections so
Wee let in nought to make them over-flow.
And as of Homers verses, many critickes
On those stand of which times old moth hath eaten
The first or last feete, and the perfect parts
Of his unmatched poeme sinke beneath,
With upright gasping and sloath dull as death:
So the unprofitable things of life,
And those we cannot compasse, we affect;
All that doth profit and wee have, neglect,
Like covetous and basely getting men
That, gathering much, use never what they keepe;
But for the least they loose, extreamely weepe.

MAILLARD
This prettie talking, and our horses walking
Downe this steepe hill, spends time with equall profit.

CLERMONT
Tis well bestow'd on ye; meate and men sicke
Agree like this and you: and yet even this
Is th'end of all skill, power, wealth, all that is.

CHALON
I long to heare, sir, how your mistresse takes this.

[Enter **AUMALE** with a cabinet.

MAILLARD
Wee soone shall know it; see Aumall return'd.

AUMALE
Ease to your bands, sir!

CLERMONT
Welcome, worthy friend!

CHALON
How tooke his noblest mistresse your sad message?

AUMALE
As great rich men take sodaine povertie.
I never witness'd a more noble love,
Nor a more ruthfull sorrow: I well wisht
Some other had beene master of my message.

MAILLARD
Y'are happy, sir, in all things, but this one
Of your unhappy apprehension.

CLERMONT
This is to mee, compar'd with her much mone,
As one teare is to her whole passion.

AUMALE
Sir, shee commends her kindest service to you,
And this rich cabinet.

CHALON
O happy man!
This may enough hold to redeeme your bands.

CLERMONT
These clouds, I doubt not, will be soone blowne over.

[Enter **BALIGNY**, with his discharge: **RENEL**, and **OTHERS**.

AUMALE
Your hope is just and happy; see, sir, both
In both the looks of these.

BALIGNY
Here's a discharge

For this your prisoner, my good Lord Lieutenant.

MAILLARD
Alas, sir, I usurpe that stile, enforc't,
And hope you know it was not my aspiring.

BALIGNY
Well, sir, my wrong aspir'd past all mens hopes.

MAILLARD
I sorrow for it, sir.

RENEL
You see, sir, there
Your prisoners discharge autenticall.

MAILLARD
It is, sir, and I yeeld it him with gladnesse.

BALIGNY
Brother, I brought you downe to much good purpose.

CLERMONT
Repeate not that, sir; the amends makes all.

RENEL
I joy in it, my best and worthiest friend;
O, y'have a princely fautor of the Guise.

BALIGNY
I thinke I did my part to.

RENEL
Well, sir, all
Is in the issue well: and (worthiest friend)
Here's from your friend, the Guise; here from the Countesse,
Your brothers mistresse, the contents whereof
I know, and must prepare you now to please
Th'unrested spirit of your slaughtered brother,
If it be true, as you imagin'd once,
His apparition show'd it. The complot
Is now laid sure betwixt us; therefore haste
Both to your great friend (who hath some use waightie
For your repaire to him) and to the Countesse,
Whose satisfaction is no lesse important.

CLERMONT
I see all, and will haste as it importeth.

And good friend, since I must delay a little
My wisht attendance on my noblest mistresse,
Excuse me to her, with returne of this,
And endlesse protestation of my service;
And now become as glad a messenger,
As you were late a wofull.

AUMALE
Happy change!
I ever will salute thee with my service.

[Exit.

BALIGNY
Yet more newes, brother; the late jesting Monsieur
Makes now your brothers dying prophesie equall
At all parts, being dead as he presag'd.

RENEL
Heaven shield the Guise from seconding that truth
With what he likewise prophesied on him!

CLERMONT
It hath enough, twas grac'd with truth in one;
To'th other falshood and confusion!
Leade to the Court, sir.

BALIGNY
You lle leade no more;
It was to ominous and foule before.

[Exeunt.

ACTUS QUINTI

SCÆNA PRIMA

A Room in the Palace of the Duke of Guise

Ascendit **UMBRA BUSSI**.

UMBRA BUSSI
Up from the chaos of eternall night
(To which the whole digestion of the world
Is now returning) once more I ascend,
And bide the cold dampe of this piercing ayre,

To urge the justice whose almightie word
Measures the bloudy acts of impious men
With equall pennance, who in th'act it selfe
Includes th'infliction, which like chained shot
Batter together still; though (as the thunder
Seemes, by mens duller hearing then their sight,
To breake a great time after lightning forth,
Yet both at one time teare the labouring cloud)
So men thinke pennance of their ils is slow,
Though th'ill and pennance still together goe.
Reforme, yee ignorant men, your manlesse lives
Whose lawes yee thinke are nothing but your lusts;
When leaving (but for supposition sake)
The body of felicitie, religion,
Set in the midst of Christendome, and her head
Cleft to her bosome, one halfe one way swaying,
Another th'other, all the Christian world
And all her lawes whose observation
Stands upon faith, above the power of reason—
Leaving (I say) all these, this might suffice
To fray yee from your vicious swindge in ill
And set you more on fire to doe more good;
That since the world (as which of you denies?)
Stands by proportion, all may thence conclude
That all the joynts and nerves sustaining nature
As well may breake, and yet the world abide,
As any one good unrewarded die,
Or any one ill scape his penaltie.

[The **GHOST** stands close.

[Enter **GUISE, CLERMONT**.

GUISE
Thus friend thou seest how all good men would thrive,
Did not the good thou prompt'st me with prevent
The jealous ill pursuing them in others.
But now thy dangers are dispatcht, note mine.
Hast thou not heard of that admired voyce
That at the barricadoes spake to mee,
(No person seene) "Let's leade my lord to Reimes"?

CLERMONT
Nor could you learne the person?

GUISE
By no meanes.

CLERMONT

Twas but your fancie, then, a waking dreame:
For as in sleepe, which bindes both th'outward senses
And the sense common to, th'imagining power
(Stird up by formes hid in the memories store,
Or by the vapours of o'er-flowing humours
In bodies full and foule, and mixt with spirits)
Faines many strange, miraculous images,
In which act it so painfully applyes
It selfe to those formes that the common sense
It actuates with his motion, and thereby
Those fictions true seeme and have reall act:
So, in the strength of our conceits awake,
The cause alike doth oft like fictions make.

GUISE

Be what it will, twas a presage of something
Waightie and secret, which th'advertisements
I have receiv'd from all parts, both without
And in this kingdome, as from Rome and Spaine,
Lorraine and Savoye, gives me cause to thinke,
All writing that our plots catastrophe,
For propagation of the Catholique cause,
Will bloudy prove, dissolving all our counsailes.

CLERMONT

Retyre, then, from them all.

GUISE

I must not doe so.
The Arch-Bishop of Lyons tels me plaine
I shall be said then to abandon France
In so important an occasion;
And that mine enemies (their profit making
Of my faint absence) soone would let that fall,
That all my paines did to this height exhale.

CLERMONT

Let all fall that would rise unlawfully!
Make not your forward spirit in vertues right
A property for vice, by thrusting on
Further then all your powers can fetch you off.
It is enough, your will is infinite
To all things vertuous and religious,
Which, within limits kept, may without danger
Let vertue some good from your graces gather.
Avarice of all is ever nothings father.

UMBRA

Danger (the spurre of all great mindes) is ever
The curbe to your tame spirits; you respect not
(With all your holinesse of life and learning)
More then the present, like illiterate vulgars;
Your minde (you say) kept in your fleshes bounds
Showes that mans will must rul'd be by his power:
When by true doctrine you are taught to live
Rather without the body then within,
And rather to your God still then your selfe.
To live to Him is to doe all things fitting
His image in which like Himselfe we live;
To be His image is to doe those things
That make us deathlesse, which by death is onely
Doing those deedes that fit eternitie;
And those deedes are the perfecting that justice
That makes the world last, which proportion is
Of punishment and wreake for every wrong,
As well as for right a reward as strong:
Away, then! use the meanes thou hast to right
The wrong I suffer'd. What corrupted law
Leaves unperform'd in Kings, doe thou supply,
And be above them all in dignitie.

[Exit.

GUISE

Why stand'st thou still thus, and applyest thine eares
And eyes to nothing?

CLERMONT

Saw you nothing here?

GUISE

Thou dream'st awake now; what was here to see?

CLERMONT

My brothers spirit, urging his revenge.

GUISE

Thy brothers spirit! pray thee mocke me not.

CLERMONT

No, by my love and service.

GUISE

Would he rise,
And not be thundring threates against the Guise?

CLERMONT

You make amends for enmitie to him,
With tenne parts more love and desert of mee;
And as you make your hate to him no let
Of any love to mee, no more beares hee
(Since you to me supply it) hate to you.
Which reason and which justice is perform'd
In spirits tenne parts more then fleshy men;
To whose fore-sights our acts and thoughts lie open:
And therefore, since hee saw the treacherie
Late practis'd by my brother Baligny,
Hee would not honor his hand with the justice
(As hee esteemes it) of his blouds revenge,
To which my sister needes would have him sworne,
Before she would consent to marry him.

GUISE

O Baligny!—who would beleeve there were
A man that (onely since his lookes are rais'd
Upwards, and have but sacred heaven in sight)
Could beare a minde so more then divellish?
As for the painted glory of the countenance,
Flitting in Kings, doth good for nought esteeme,
And the more ill hee does, the better seeme.

CLERMONT

Wee easily may beleeve it, since we see
In this worlds practise few men better be.
Justice to live doth nought but justice neede,
But policie must still on mischiefe feede.
Untruth, for all his ends, truths name doth sue in;
None safely live but those that study ruine.
A good man happy is a common good;
Ill men advanc'd live of the common bloud.

GUISE

But this thy brothers spirit startles mee,
These spirits seld or never hanting men
But some mishap ensues.

CLERMONT

Ensue what can;
Tyrants may kill but never hurt a man;
All to his good makes, spight of death and hell.

[Enter **AUMALE.**

AUMALE
All the desert of good renowne your Highnesse!

GUISE
Welcome, Aumall!

CLERMONT
My good friend, friendly welcome!
How tooke my noblest mistresse the chang'd newes?

AUMALE
It came too late sir, for those loveliest eyes
(Through which a soule look't so divinely loving,
Teares nothing uttering her distresse enough)
She wept quite out, and, like two falling starres,
Their dearest sights quite vanisht with her teares.

CLERMONT
All good forbid it!

GUISE
What events are these!

CLERMONT
All must be borne, my lord; and yet this chance
Would willingly enforce a man to cast off
All power to beare with comfort, since hee sees
In this our comforts made our miseries.

GUISE
How strangely thou art lov'd of both the sexes;
Yet thou lov'st neyther, but the good of both.

CLERMONT
In love of women my affection first
Takes fire out of the fraile parts of my bloud;
Which, till I have enjoy'd, is passionate
Like other lovers; but, fruition past,
I then love out of judgement, the desert
Of her I love still sticking in my heart,
Though the desire and the delight be gone,
Which must chance still, since the comparison
Made upon tryall twixt what reason loves,
And what affection, makes in mee the best
Ever preferd, what most love, valuing lest.

GUISE
Thy love being judgement then, and of the minde,

Marry thy worthiest mistresse now being blinde.

CLERMONT
If there were love in mariage, so I would;
But I denie that any man doth love,
Affecting wives, maides, widowes, any women:
For neither flyes love milke, although they drowne
In greedy search thereof; nor doth the bee
Love honey, though the labour of her life
Is spent in gathering it; nor those that fat
On beasts, or fowles, doe any thing therein
For any love: for as when onely nature
Moves men to meate, as farre as her power rules,
Shee doth it with a temperate appetite,
The too much men devoure abhorring nature,
And in our most health is our most disease:
So, when humanitie rules men and women,
Tis for societie confinde in reason.
But what excites the beds desire in bloud,
By no meanes justly can be construed love;
For when love kindles any knowing spirit,
It ends in vertue and effects divine,
And is in friendship chaste and masculine.

GUISE
Thou shalt my mistresse be; me thinkes my bloud
Is taken up to all love with thy vertues.
And howsoever other men despise
These paradoxes strange and too precise,
Since they hold on the right way of our reason,
I could attend them ever. Come, away;
Performe thy brothers thus importun'd wreake;
And I will see what great affaires the King
Hath to employ my counsell which he seemes
Much to desire, and more and more esteemes.

[Exeunt.

SCÆNA SECUNDA

A Room at the Court

Enter **HENRY, BALIGNY**, with **SIX** of the **GUARD**.

HENRY
Saw you his sawcie forcing of my hand

To D'Ambois freedome?

BALIGNY

Saw, and through mine eyes
Let fire into my heart, that burn'd to beare
An insolence so giantly austere.

HENRY

The more Kings beare at subjects hands, the more
Their lingring justice gathers; that resembles
The waightie and the goodly-bodied eagle,
Who (being on earth) before her shady wings
Can raise her into ayre, a mightie way
Close by the ground she runnes; but being aloft,
All shee commands, she flyes at; and the more
Death in her seres beares, the more time shee stayes
Her thundry stoope from that on which shee preyes.

BALIGNY

You must be then more secret in the waight
Of these your shadie counsels, who will else
Beare (where such sparkes flye as the Guise and D'Ambois)
Pouder about them. Counsels (as your entrailes)
Should be unpierst and sound kept; for not those
Whom you discover you neglect; but ope
A ruinous passage to your owne best hope.

HENRY

Wee have spies set on us, as we on others;
And therefore they that serve us must excuse us,
If what wee most hold in our hearts take winde;
Deceit hath eyes that see into the minde.
But this plot shall be quicker then their twinckling,
On whose lids Fate with her dead waight shall lie,
And confidence that lightens ere she die.
Friends of my Guard, as yee gave othe to be
True to your Soveraigne, keepe it manfully.
Your eyes have witnest oft th'ambition
That never made accesse to me in Guise
But treason ever sparkled in his eyes;
Which if you free us of, our safetie shall
You not our subjects but our patrons call.

OMNES

Our duties binde us; hee is now but dead.

HENRY

Wee trust in it, and thanke ye. Baligny,

Goe lodge their ambush, and thou God, that art
Fautor of princes, thunder from the skies
Beneath his hill of pride this gyant Guise.

[Exeunt.

SCÆNA TERTIA

A Room in Montsurry's House

Enter **TAMYRA** with a letter, **CHARLOTTE** in man's attire.

TAMYRA
I see y'are servant, sir, to my deare sister,
The lady of her loved Baligny.

CHARLOTTE
Madame, I am bound to her vertuous bounties
For that life which I offer, in her service,
To the revenge of her renowned brother.

TAMYRA
She writes to mee as much, and much desires
That you may be the man, whose spirit shee knowes
Will cut short off these long and dull delayes
Hitherto bribing the eternall Justice:
Which I beleeve, since her unmatched spirit
Can judge of spirits that have her sulphure in them.
But I must tell you that I make no doubt
Her living brother will revenge her dead,
On whom the dead impos'd the taske, and hee,
I know, will come t'effect it instantly.

CHARLOTTE
They are but words in him; beleeve them not.

TAMYRA
See; this is the vault where he must enter;
Where now I thinke hee is.

[Enter **RENEL** at the vault, with the **COUNTESS** being blinde.

RENEL
God save you, lady!
What gentleman is this, with whom you trust
The deadly waightie secret of this houre?

TAMYRA
One that your selfe will say I well may trust.

RENEL
Then come up, madame.

[He helps the **COUNTESS** up.

See here, honour'd lady,
A Countesse that in loves mishap doth equall
At all parts your wrong'd selfe, and is the mistresse
Of your slaine servants brother; in whose love,
For his late treachrous apprehension,
She wept her faire eyes from her ivory browes,
And would have wept her soule out, had not I
Promist to bring her to this mortall quarrie,
That by her lost eyes for her servants love
She might conjure him from this sterne attempt,
In which (by a most ominous dreame shee had)
Shee knowes his death fixt, and that never more
Out of this place the sunne shall see him live.

CHARLOTTE
I am provided, then, to take his place
And undertaking on me.

RENEL
You sir, why?

CHARLOTTE
Since I am charg'd so by my mistresse,
His mournfull sister.

TAMYRA
See her letter, sir.

[He reades.

Good madame, I rue your fate more then mine,
And know not how to order these affaires,
They stand on such occurrents.

RENEL
This, indeede,
I know to be your lady mistresse hand;
And know besides, his brother will and must
Indure no hand in this revenge but his.

Enter **UMBRA BUSSY**.

UMBRA
Away, dispute no more; get up, and see!
Clermont must auchthor this just tragedie.

COUNTESS
Who's that?

RENEL
The spirit of Bussy.

TAMYRA
O my servant!
Let us embrace.

UMBRA
Forbeare! The ayre, in which
My figures liknesse is imprest, will blast.
Let my revenge for all loves satisfie,
In which, dame, feare not, Clermont shall not dye.
No word dispute more; up, and see th'event.

[Exeunt **LADYES**.

Make the guard sure, Renel; and then the doores
Command to make fast, when the Earle is in.

[Exit **RENEL**.

The blacke soft-footed houre is now on wing,
Which, for my just wreake, ghosts shall celebrate
With dances dire and of infernall state.

[Exit.

SCÆNA QUARTA

An Ante-room to the Council-Chamber

Enter **GUISE**.

GUISE
Who sayes that death is naturall, when nature
Is with the onely thought of it dismaid?

I have had lotteries set up for my death,
And I have drawne beneath my trencher one,
Knit in my hand-kerchiefe another lot,
The word being, "Y'are a dead man if you enter";
And these words this imperfect bloud and flesh
Shrincke at in spight of me, their solidst part
Melting like snow within mee with colde fire.
I hate my selfe, that, seeking to rule Kings,
I cannot curbe my slave. Would any spirit
Free, manly, princely, wish to live to be
Commanded by this masse of slaverie,
Since reason, judgement, resolution,
And scorne of what we feare, will yeeld to feare?
While this same sincke of sensualitie swels,
Who would live sinking in it? and not spring
Up to the starres, and leave this carrion here,
For wolfes, and vultures, and for dogges to teare?
O Clermont D'Ambois, wert thou here to chide
This softnesse from my flesh, farre as my reason,
Farre as my resolution not to stirre
One foote out of the way for death and hell!
Let my false man by falshood perish here;
There's no way else to set my true man cleere.

[Enter **MESSENGER**.

MESSENGER
The King desires your Grace to come to Councill.

GUISE
I come. It cannot be; hee will not dare
To touch me with a treacherie so prophane.
Would Clermont now were here, to try how hee
Would lay about him, if this plot should be:
Here would be tossing soules into the skie.
Who ever knew bloud sav'd by treacherie?
Well, I must on, and will; what should I feare?
Not against two, Alcides; against two,
And Hercules to friend, the Guise will goe.

[He takes up the Arras, and the **GUARD** enters upon him: he drawes.

GUISE
Holde, murtherers!

[They strike him downe.

So then, this is confidence

In greatnes, not in goodnes. Wher is the King?

[The **KING** comes in sight with **ESPERONE, SOISSONE**, and **OTHERS**.

Let him appeare to justifie his deede,
In spight of my betrai'd wounds; ere my soule
Take her flight through them, and my tongue hath strength
To urge his tyrannie.

HENRY
See, sir, I am come
To justifie it before men and God,
Who knowes with what wounds in my heart for woe
Of your so wounded faith I made these wounds,
Forc't to it by an insolence of force
To stirre a stone; nor is a rocke, oppos'd
To all the billowes of the churlish sea,
More beate and eaten with them then was I
With your ambitious, mad idolatrie;
And this bloud I shed is to save the bloud
Of many thousands.

GUISE
That's your white pretext;
But you will finde one drop of bloud shed lawlesse
Will be the fountaine to a purple sea.
The present lust and shift made for Kings lives,
Against the pure forme and just power of law,
Will thrive like shifters purchases; there hangs
A blacke starre in the skies, to which the sunne
Gives yet no light, will raine a poyson'd shower
Into your entrailes, that will make you feele
How little safetie lies in treacherous steele.

HENRY
Well, sir, Ile beare it; y'have a brother to
Bursts with like threates, the skarlet Cardinall—
Seeke, and lay hands on him; and take this hence,
Their blouds, for all you, on my conscience!

[Exit.

GUISE
So, sir, your full swindge take; mine death hath curb'd.
Clermont, farewell! O didst thou see but this!
But it is better; see by this the ice
Broke to thine owne bloud, which thou wilt despise
When thou hear'st mine shed. Is there no friend here

Will beare my love to him?

AUMALE
I will, my lord.

GUISE
Thankes with my last breath: recommend me, then,
To the most worthy of the race of men.

[Dyes. Exeunt.

SCÆNA QUINTA

A Room in Montsurry's House

Enter **MONTSURRY** and **TAMYRA**.

MONTSURRY
Who have you let into my house?

TAMYRA
I? none.

MONTSURRY
Tis false; I savour the rancke bloud of foes
In every corner.

TAMYRA
That you may doe well;
It is the bloud you lately shed you smell.

MONTSURRY
Sdeath! the vault opens.

[The gulfe opens.

TAMYRA
What vault? hold your sword.

[**CLERMONT** ascends.

CLERMONT
No, let him use it.

MONTSURRY
Treason! murther! murther!

CLERMONT
Exclaime not; tis in vaine, and base in you,
Being one to onely one.

MONTSURRY
O bloudy strumpet!

CLERMONT
With what bloud charge you her? it may be mine
As well as yours; there shall not any else
Enter or touch you: I conferre no guards,
Nor imitate the murtherous course you tooke,
But single here will have my former challenge
Now answer'd single; not a minute more
My brothers bloud shall stay for his revenge,
If I can act it; if not, mine shall adde
A double conquest to you, that alone
Put it to fortune now, and use no ods.
Storme not, nor beate your selfe thus gainst the dores,
Like to a savage vermine in a trap:
All dores are sure made, and you cannot scape
But by your valour.

MONTSURRY
No, no, come and kill mee.

CLERMONT
If you will die so like a beast, you shall;
But when the spirit of a man may save you,
Doe not so shame man, and a Nobleman.

MONTSURRY
I doe not show this basenesse that I feare thee,
But to prevent and shame thy victory,
Which of one base is base, and so Ile die.

CLERMONT
Here, then.

MONTSURRY
Stay, hold! One thought hath harden'd me,

[He starts up.

And since I must afford thee victorie,
It shall be great and brave, if one request
Thou wilt admit mee.

CLERMONT
What's that?

MONTSURRY
Give me leave
To fetch and use the sword thy brother gave mee,
When he was bravely giving up his life.

CLERMONT
No; Ile not fight against my brothers sword;
Not that I feare it, but since tis a tricke
For you to show your backe.

MONTSURRY
By all truth, no:
Take but my honourable othe, I will not.

CLERMONT
Your honourable othe! Plaine truth no place has
Where othes are honourable.

TAMYRA
Trust not his othe.
Hee will lie like a lapwing; when shee flyes
Farre from her sought nest, still "Here tis" shee cryes.

MONTSURRY
Out on thee, damme of divels! I will quite
Disgrace thy bravos conquest, die, not fight.

[Lyes downe.

TAMYRA
Out on my fortune, to wed such an abject!
Now is the peoples voyce the voyce of God;
Hee that to wound a woman vants so much,
As hee did mee, a man dares never touch.

CLERMONT
Revenge your wounds now, madame; I resigne him
Up to your full will, since hee will not fight.
First you shall torture him (as hee did you,
And justice wils) and then pay I my vow.
Here, take this ponyard.

MONTSURRY
Sinke earth, open heaven,

And let fall vengeance!

TAMYRA
Come sir, good sir, hold him.

MONTSURRY
O shame of women, whither art thou fled!

CLERMONT
Why (good my lord) is it a greater shame
For her then you? come, I will be the bands
You us'd to her, prophaning her faire hands.

MONTSURRY
No, sir, Ile fight now, and the terror be
Of all you champions to such as shee.
I did but thus farre dally; now observe.
O all you aking fore-heads that have rob'd
Your hands of weapons and your hearts of valour,
Joyne in mee all your rages and rebutters,
And into dust ram this same race of Furies;
In this one relicke of the Ambois gall,
In his one purple soule shed, drowne it all.

[Fight.

MONTSURRY
Now give me breath a while.

CLERMONT
Receive it freely.

MONTSURRY
What thinke y'a this now?

CLERMONT
It is very noble,
Had it beene free, at least, and of your selfe;
And thus wee see (where valour most doth vant)
What tis to make a coward valiant.

MONTSURRY
Now I shall grace your conquest.

CLERMONT
That you shall.

MONTSURRY

If you obtaine it.

CLERMONT
True, sir, tis in fortune.

MONTSURRY
If you were not a D'Ambois, I would scarce
Change lives with you, I feele so great a change
In my tall spirits breath'd, I thinke, with the breath
A D'Ambois breathes here; and necessitie
(With whose point now prickt on, and so whose helpe
My hands may challenge) that doth all men conquer,
If shee except not you of all men onely,
May change the case here.

CLERMONT
True, as you are chang'd;
Her power, in me urg'd, makes y'another man
Then yet you ever were.

MONTSURRY
Well, I must on.

CLERMONT
Your lordship must by all meanes.

MONTSURRY
Then at all.

[Fights, and **CLERMONT D'AMBOIS** hurts him.

[Enter **RENEL**, the **COUNTESS**, and **CHARLOTTE** above.

CHARLOTTE
Death of my father, what a shame is this!
Sticke in his hands thus!

[She gets downe.

RENEL [trying to stop her]
Gentle sir, forbeare!

COUNTESS
Is he not slaine yet?

RENEL
No, madame, but hurt
In divers parts of him.

MONTSURRY
Y'have given it me,
And yet I feele life for another vennie.

[Enter **CHARLOTTE** below.

CLERMONT
What would you, sir?

CHARLOTTE
I would performe this combat.

CLERMONT
Against which of us?

CHARLOTTE
I care not much if twere
Against thy selfe; thy sister would have sham'd
To have thy brothers wreake with any man
In single combat sticke so in her fingers.

CLERMONT
My sister! know you her?

TAMYRA
I, sir, shee sent him
With this kinde letter, to performe the wreake
Of my deare servant.

CLERMONT
Now, alas! good sir,
Thinke you you could doe more?

CHARLOTTE
Alas! I doe;
And wer't not I, fresh, sound, should charge a man
Weary and wounded, I would long ere this
Have prov'd what I presume on.

CLERMONT
Y'have a minde
Like to my sister, but have patience now;
If next charge speede not, Ile resigne to you.

MONTSURRY
Pray thee, let him decide it.

CLERMONT
No, my lord,
I am the man in fate; and since so bravely
Your lordship stands mee, scape but one more charge,
And, on my life, Ile set your life at large.

MONTSURRY
Said like a D'Ambois, and if now I die,
Sit joy and all good on thy victorie!

[Fights, and fals downe.

MONTSURRY
Farewell! I hartily forgive thee; wife,
And thee; let penitence spend thy rest of life.

[Hee gives his hand to **CLERMONT** and his **WIFE**.

CLERMONT
Noble and Christian!

TAMYRA
O, it breakes my heart.

CLERMONT
And should; for all faults found in him before
These words, this end, makes full amends and more.
Rest, worthy soule; and with it the deare spirit
Of my lov'd brother rest in endlesse peace!
Soft lie thy bones; Heaven be your soules abode;
And to your ashes be the earth no lode!

[Musicke, and the **GHOST** of Bussy enters, leading the **GHOSTS** of the Guise, Monsieur, Cardinall Guise, and Shattilion; they dance about the dead body, and exeunt.

CLERMONT
How strange is this! The Guise amongst these spirits,
And his great brother Cardinall, both yet living!
And that the rest with them with joy thus celebrate
This our revenge! This certainely presages
Some instant death both to the Guise and Cardinall.
That the Shattilions ghost to should thus joyne
In celebration of this just revenge
With Guise that bore a chiefe stroke in his death,
It seemes that now he doth approve the act;
And these true shadowes of the Guise and Cardinall,
Fore-running thus their bodies, may approve
That all things to be done, as here wee live,

Are done before all times in th'other life.
That spirits should rise in these times yet are fables;
Though learnedst men hold that our sensive spirits
A little time abide about the graves
Of their deceased bodies, and can take,
In colde condenc't ayre, the same formes they had
When they were shut up in this bodies shade.

[Enter **AUMALE**.

AUMALE
O sir, the Guise is slaine!

CLERMONT
Avert it heaven!

AUMALE
Sent for to Councill by the King, an ambush
(Lodg'd for the purpose) rusht on him, and tooke
His princely life; who sent (in dying then)
His love to you, as to the best of men.

CLERMONT
The worst and most accursed of things creeping
On earths sad bosome. Let me pray yee all
A little to forbeare, and let me use
Freely mine owne minde in lamenting him.
Ile call yee straight againe.

AUMALE
We will forbeare,
And leave you free, sir.

[Exeunt.

CLERMONT
Shall I live, and hee
Dead, that alone gave meanes of life to me?
Theres no disputing with the acts of Kings;
Revenge is impious on their sacred persons.
And could I play the worldling (no man loving
Longer then gaine is reapt or grace from him)
I should survive; and shall be wondred at
Though (in mine owne hands being) I end with him:
But friendship is the sement of two mindes,
As of one man the soule and body is,
Of which one cannot sever but the other
Suffers a needfull separation.

RENEL
I feare your servant, madame: let's descend.

[Descend **RENEL** and **COUNTESS**.

CLERMONT
Since I could skill of man, I never liv'd
To please men worldly, and shall I in death
Respect their pleasures, making such a jarre
Betwixt my death and life, when death should make
The consort sweetest, th'end being proofe and crowne
To all the skill and worth wee truely owne?
Guise, O my lord, how shall I cast from me
The bands and coverts hindring me from thee?
The garment or the cover of the minde
The humane soule is; of the soule, the spirit
The proper robe is; of the spirit, the bloud;
And of the bloud, the body is the shrowd.
With that must I beginne then to unclothe,
And come at th'other. Now, then, as a ship
Touching at strange and farre removed shores,
Her men a shore goe, for their severall ends,
Fresh water, victuals, precious stones, and pearle,
All yet intentive, when the master cals,
The ship to put off ready, to leave all
Their greediest labours, lest they there be left
To theeves or beasts, or be the countries slaves:
So, now my master cals, my ship, my venture
All in one bottome put, all quite put off,
Gone under saile, and I left negligent
To all the horrors of the vicious time,
The farre remov'd shores to all vertuous aimes,
None favouring goodnesse, none but he respecting
Pietie or man-hood—shall I here survive,
Not cast me after him into the sea,
Rather then here live, readie every houre
To feede theeves, beasts, and be the slave of power?
I come, my lord! Clermont, thy creature, comes.

[He kils himselfe.

[Enter **AUMALE, TAMYRA, CHARLOTTE**.

AUMALE
What! lye and languish, Clermont! Cursed man,
To leave him here thus! hee hath slaine himselfe.

TAMYRA

Misery on misery! O me wretched dame,
Of all that breath! all heaven turne all his eyes
In harty envie thus on one poore dame.

CHARLOTTE

Well done, my brother! I did love thee ever,
But now adore thee: losse of such a friend
None should survive, of such a brother none.
With my false husband live, and both these slaine!
Ere I returne to him, Ile turne to earth.

[Enter **RENEL** leading the **COUNTESS**.

RENEL

Horror of humane eyes! O Clermont D'Ambois!
Madame, wee staid too long, your servant's slaine.

COUNTESS

It must be so; he liv'd but in the Guise,
As I in him. O follow life mine eyes!

TAMYRA

Hide, hide thy snakie head; to cloisters flie;
In pennance pine; too easie tis to die.

CHARLOTTE

It is. In cloisters then let's all survive.
Madame, since wrath nor griefe can helpe these fortunes,
Let us forsake the world in which they raigne,
And for their wisht amends to God complaine.

COUNTESS

Tis fit and onely needfull: leade me on;
In heavens course comfort seeke, in earth is none.

[Exeunt.

[Enter **HENRY, ESPERONE, SOISSONE,** and **OTHERS**.

HENRY

Wee came indeede too late, which much I rue,
And would have kept this Clermont as my crowne.
Take in the dead, and make this fatall roome
(The house shut up) the famous D'Ambois tombe.

[Exeunt.

DE LA MORT PITOYABLE DU VALEUREUX LYSIS

Under this title, in the 17th of the series of tales founded on fact which he calls Les Histoires Tragiques de Nostre Temps, François de Rosset relates in 1615 the story of Bussy's death. In the Preface to the volume he declares: "Ce ne sont pas des contes de l'Antiquité fabuleuse . . . Ce sont des histoires autant veritables que tristes et funestes. Les noms de la pluspart des personnages sont seulement desguisez en ce Théatre, à fin de n'affliger pas tant les familles de ceux qui en ont donné le suject, puis qu'elles en sont assez affligées." We thus find that the outlines of the story of "Lysis" tally with what we know about Bussy from other sources, and Rosset not improbably preserves details omitted by the historians of the period.

Lysis, Rosset tells us, was sprung from one of the most noble and renowned Houses of France. At seventeen he had acquired an extraordinary reputation for bravery, which increased till "jamais la France depuis le valeureux Roland, ne porta un tel Palladin." Afterwards "il vint à la cour du Prince qui venoit de quiter une Couronne estrangere, pour recevoir celle qui luy appartenoit par les droits de la loy Salique, [i. e. Henry III, who gave up the throne of Poland on succeeding to that of France.] . . . Les rares dons dont il estoit accomply luy acquirent tant de part aux bonnes graces du premier Prince du sang Royal, qu'il estoit tousiours aupres de luy. . . . Mais l'envie . . . tous les jours . . . faisait de mauvais rapports a sa Maiesté de Lysis, de sorte qu'elle le voyoit d'aussi mauvais oeil, que l'autre Prince, son proche parent, faisoit conte de sa prouësse."

He had never been the victim of love, but he was instantly captivated by the beautiful eyes of a lady whom he met at an assembly at the house of a Judge in one of the towns of which he was Governor.

"Ceste beauté, pour le respect que je dois à ceux a qui elle appartenoit, sera nommée Sylvie. . . . Cette dame . . . estoit mariée avec un grand Seigneur, jeune, vaillan, sage, discret et courtois." She would not at first gratify her lover's passion, though she granted him "de petites privautez," which only fanned the flame. He wrote her a letter in which he declared that if she refused him her favour, it meant his sentence of death. She replied in a temporising manner that when he had given proofs of his fidelity, she would decide as to what she ought to do. Rosset asserts that these two letters are not invented, but that he obtained them from a friend who had made a collection of such epistles, and who "a esté curieux de sçavoir le nom des personnes qui les ont escrites."

Meanwhile, he continues, "elle donne le vray moyen à Lysis de la voir, sans le souciet qu'on en parle, pourveu que sa conscience la deffende. Et particulierement ce fut en un jardin qui est à l'un des fauxbourgs de la ville." Some tale-bearers, putting the worst construction on their behaviour, gave information to Lisandre, the husband of Sylvie, but he refused to credit anything to the dishonour of his wife. To stop gossip, however, he took her with him to a house he had not far from the town. But the lovers communicated with one another by messengers, till Lisandre's departure on a journey removed all obstacle to their intercourse. "Ce Seigneur avait des affaires hors de la province où il faisoit pour lors sa demeure. Pour les terminer, il s'y achemine au grand contentement de Sylvie, qui neantmoins contrefaisoit la dolente à son depart & le sommoit de revenir le plustot qu'il luy seroit possible, tandis que dans son ame elle prioit à Dieu que son voyage fust aussi long que celuy d'Ulysse." When he was gone, she immediately sent for Lysis, and they spent two or three days in transports of delight, though she continued to safeguard her honour.

On Lisandre's return the King, instigated by the enemies of Lysis, reproached the former for tamely enduring dishonour, and bade him never reappear in the royal presence till he had wiped out the stain. Lisandre therefore offered his wife the choice of three courses. She was to swallow poison, or die beneath his dagger, or write to Lysis, telling him that Lisandre was still absent, and begging him to come to her. After a struggle Sylvie wrote the fatal missive, and Lysis, though at the castle gate he was overcome by a premonition of evil and almost turned back, was obedient to her summons, and entered her chamber unarmed. The final scene is thus described.

"A l'instant il se void environné d'une douzaine d'hommes armez, qui de pistolets, qui d'espees nues, et qui de hallebardes. Lisandre est parmy eux, qui luy crie: 'C'est maintenant que tu recevras le salaire de la honte que tu as faicte à ma maison. Ce disant, il lasche un pistolet, et luy perce un bras. Les autres le chargent avec leurs halebardes, et avec leurs espees. . . . Le valeureux Lysis . . . avec un escabeau qu'il tient en main donne si rudement sur la teste de l'un de ses adversaires, qu'il en fait sortir la cervelle. Il en assomme encores deux autres: mais que peut-il faire contre tant de gens, & ainsi desarmé qu'il est? Son corps percé comme un crible, verse un grand ruisseau de sang. En fin il se jette sur Lisandre, et bien que par derriere on luy baille cent coups de poignards, il le prend, et le souleve, prest à le jetter du haut en bas d'une fenestre, si tous les autres ensemble, en se jettant sur luy, ne l'en eussent empesché. Il les escarte encores à coups de poings & neantmoins il sesent tousiours percer de part en part. Voyant qu'il ne pouvoit eschapper la mort, il s'approche de la fenestre & puis, tout sanglant qu'il est, il saute legerement en bas. Mais, ô malheur, il portoit un accoustrement decouppé, qui est arresté par le fer d'un treillis. Ses adversaires le voyant ainsi empestré comme un autre Absalon, luy donnent tant de coups de halebardes, qu'à la fin, ils privent le monde du plus grand courage, et de la plus grande valeur du siecle. O valeureux Lysis! que je plains l'injustice de ton sort!"

It will be seen that Rosset's account of the final episodes, beginning with the intervention of the King, agrees, in the main details, with the following description by De Thou, which appeared in 1620, in the Genevan edition of the Historiae Sui Temporis, lib. LXVIII, p. 330 (vol. III, p. 675, of Buckley's edition, 1733).

"Dum[*] adhuc Andinus in aula esset, literas per jocum regi ostenderat a Ludovico Claramontio Ambosiano Bussio ad se scriptas; quibus, pro summa quae ei cum hero suo juvene erat familiaritate, significabat se feram magni venatoris (ita uxorem vocabat Caroli Cambii Monsorelli comitis, quem ea dignitate Andinus paulo ante Bussii commendatione ornaverat) indagine cinxisse, et in plagas conjecisse. Quas literas rex retinuerat, et Bussii jam a longo tempore insolenti arrogantia et petulantia irritatus, occasionem inde sumpsit veteres ab eo acceptas injurias ulciscendi. Is siquidem, et dum in aula esset, nullo non contumeliae genere in proceres et gynaeceum etiam aulicum usus fuerat, fiducia pugnacitatis qua se terribilem cunctis reddiderat; sed etiam postquam se ad comitatum Andini receperat, dum Andegavi arcem toto illo tractu munitissimam et urbi populosae impositam teneret, oppidanis et toti provinciae gravis ob crebras exactiones, quas privata auctoritate, non consulto plerumque Andino ipso, faciebat, summum omnium odium in se concitaverat. Igitur rex Monsorellum, qui tunc forte in aula erat, clam revocat, et literas Bussii ei ostendit; additque se decoris familiae et ejus dignitatis perquam studiosum, noluisse rem adeo injuriosam eum celare; ceterum scire ipsum debere, quid consilii in tali occasione se capere deceat et oporteat. Nec plura elocutus hominem dimittit, qui, non solum injuriae tantae morsu perculsus, sed monitis regis incitatus, quae ille tanquam ignaviae exprobationem si injuriam ferret accipiebat, protinus domum revolat, summo silentio, ut Bussium lateret: astuque per uxorem ad Bussium literas dari curat, quibus ei horam ad secretum Coustanteriae condicebat; ea erat arx voluptuaria et venationibus opportuna; ad quam cum Bussius cum Colladone conscio sub vesperam XIV Kal. Sept. venisset, ab ipso Monsorello et aliis loricatis oppressus: tamen, qua erat animi praesentia, quamvis unus contra plures, summa vi percussores initio disjecit; tandemque numero victus, spiritu inter certandum deficiente, cum se in fossam per fenestram praecipitare vellet, a tergo interfectus est."

FOOTNOTES:

*While the Duke of Anjou was still at Court, he had shown in jest to the King, a letter which had been written to him by Louis de Clermont Bussy d'Ambois. In this letter, owing to the very intimate terms on which he stood with his young patron, he told him that he had enclosed and caught in his net the hind of a mighty hunter. Thus he termed the wife of Charles de Chambes, Count of Montsoreau, on whom the Duke had conferred that title a short time before, at the recommendation of Bussy. This letter the King had kept, and as he had long been annoyed by Bussy's insolent arrogance and his petulant temper, he availed himself of this opportunity of avenging the old insults he had received from him. Even while he was at Court, he had been guilty of every sort of insult to nobles and Court ladies, trusting to his prowess as a swordsman, by which he made himself a terror to every one. So also after he had betaken himself to the district of Anjou, occupying, as he did, the citadel of Angers, the most powerful stronghold in all that district, and commanding the populous city, he had made himself a burden to the townspeople and the whole province by his frequent exactions, generally made on his own authority, without consulting the Duke of Anjou. He had thus stirred up against himself a deep-seated and universal hatred.

Therefore the King secretly called aside Montsoreau, who was then at Court, and showed him Bussy's letter, and added that, as he was extremely solicitous about his family honour and his dignity, he did not wish to conceal so insulting a matter from him; for the rest he ought to know himself what measures it behoved him to take under such circumstances. Without further words he dismissed Montsoreau. The Count, stung to the quick by so grave an injury to his honour, and excited by the admonitions of the King, which he interpreted as reproaches for his cowardice, should he tamely bear the insult, at once flew home, in the greatest secrecy, so that Bussy should not know of his return. By a stratagem he arranged that a letter should be sent by his wife to Bussy, making a secret assignation with him at La Coutancière, which was a pleasure-resort and convenient for hunting purposes. When Bussy came there with his associate Colasseau at nightfall on the nineteenth of August, he was fallen upon by Montsoreau and other armed men. Yet, such was his coolness, that though he was one against many, he at first by mighty exertions discomfited his assailants. At length, overcome by numbers, and breath failing him in the struggle, he tried to throw himself out of the window into the castle-moat, but was stabbed in the back and killed.

GLOSSARY

absolute = perfect.
abus'd = deceived.
additions = titles.
admiration = wonder.
advis'd = cautious, wary.
affect = desire.

allow = allow'd = approve, approved.
amazes = bewilders.
annoy = injure.
antickes = buffoons.
apishnesse = ridiculous imitation.
approves = proves.
Argosea = a large trading vessel.
arguments = proofs.
auchthor = be the agent of.
autenticall = legally valid.
avise = intelligence.
bare = bareheaded.
barks = outer coverings.
basilisks = fabulous reptiles, whose glance was supposed to be fatal.
battailia = order of battle.
belly-gods = gluttons.
brack = breach.
brave = braverie = fine, finery.
bumbast = n., padding.
bumbasts = vb., stuffs out.
case = skin.
cast = (1) p. p., cast off, disused; (2) vb., conjecture.
censure = judge.
challenge = claim.
characters = outward symbols.
check(e) at = (1) take offence at; (2) go in pursuit of. Used technically of a hawk which turns aside from its proper quarry to follow inferior game.
clear = pure, innocent.
close = secret.
coast = travel in circuitous fashion.
colour = pretence.
comfortable = comforting.
companion = base fellow.
conceit = conception, thought.
confirm'd = well-regulated.
consent = sympathy.
contemptfull = contemptible.
cries clinke = strikes the favourable hour.
curious = careful, scrupulous.
decent = appropriate.
denizond = naturalized.
designements = arrangements.
discover = reveal.
disparking = turning park-land into plough-land.
emply = imply.
encompast = taken at a disadvantage.
enseame = bring together, introduce. Cf. Spens. F. Q. IV, II, 35-6, where the word = "includes," "contains together."

errant = productive of wandering.
events = issues.
exhale = draw up, raise.
exhalations = meteors (cf. Jul. Cæsar, II, i, 44).
explicate = unfold.
expugn'd = taken by storm.
exquire = find out.
facts = deeds.
fautor = patron.
fivers = variant of fibres.
fleerings = sneers.
forfeit = fault.
foutre = an exclamation of contempt.
fray = frighten.
giddinesse = foolhardiness.
glorious = swelling, boastful.
Gordian = Gordian knot.
graduate = rise by steps.
grasse = graze.
ackster = a prostitute's gallant or protector.
haie = a boisterous country dance.
heartlesse = cowardly.
humourous = full of humours, variable in temper.
idols = images, counterfeits.
ill-favour'd = of unpleasant appearance.
impe = piece out. Used, originally, in hawking, of the process of grafting new feathers on a maimed wing.
implide = variant of employed.
inennerable = indescribable.
informed = moulded, fashioned.
ingenuous = discerning; used mistakenly for ingenious.
injurious = insulting.
innative = native.
intelligencers = spies.
jealousie = suspicion.
jet = strut.
jiggs = farces, jocular performances.
last = a certain weight or quantity of goods. In the case of powder, it represented twenty-four barrels.
let = hinder, prevent.
limit = limitation.
lucerns = hunting dogs. Used in the same sense by Chapman in trans. of Iliad, XI, 417. The usual meaning of the word is lynx.
mall'd = beaten with a mall or mallet, crushed.
manlessly = inhumanly.
maritorious = over-fond of a husband.
mate = match oneself against.
meane = moderation.
mezel'd = leprous, fr. M. E. mesel, < O. F. mesel, mezel, leper, < M. L. misellus, a wretched person.

mere = complete.

misers = wretched persons.

moon-calves = false conceptions.

naps = glossy surfaces on cloth.

naturalls = idiots.

nice = dainty, scrupulous.

nick = notch.

novation = revolution.

openarses = medlars.

ostents = manifestations.

part = depart.

pedisequus = (Lat.) lackey.

peece = firearm, gun.

period = conclusion.

politicall = scheming.

pide = dressed in motley.

prevented = anticipated.

pricksong = music written down with points.

proof = firmness, impenetrability.

put-ofs = excuses.

queich = thicket.

quicke = alive.

randon = earlier and more correct form of random, O. F. randon f. randir, to run fast.

ready = dressed.

rebating = blunting.

rebatoes = ruffs.

rebutters = rejoinders.

reminiscion = remembrance.

remission = forgiveness.

resolv'd = informed.

revoke = call back.

rivality = rivalry.

scapes = escapades.

secureness = carelessness.

seres = claws.

sensive = endowed with sensation.

servant = lover.

several = separate.

shadowes = sunshades, or broad-brimmed hats.

shifters = tricksters, rogues.

skittish = changeable, capricious.

sooth = confirm, approve of.

spice = piece, kind.

spinners = spiders.

splinted = supported.

standish = inkstand.

stillado = rare variant of stiletto.

still'd = distilled.

strappl'd = strapped.
successe = result.
surcharg'd = overladen, vanquished.
swindge = n., sway.
swindging = swinging to and fro.
tall = excellent, brave.
temper = regulate.
touch = censure.
toy = whim.
tracts = tracks, traces.
train = stratagem.
triumphs = pageants.
troe = an exclamation of surprise, added after a question.
trumpet = trumpeter.
trusse = seize (used specially of birds of prey).
warning peece = a shot discharged as a signal.
weather = tempestuous commotion.
weed = garment.
witty = intelligent.
wrack = wreck.
wreak = revenge.
unready = undressed.
vennie = bout at fencing.

George Chapman – A Short Biography

George Chapman was born at Hitchin in Hertfordshire in about 1559. There is some evidence that Chapman attended Oxford University but did not obtain a degree, but the evidence is rather scant.

For most of his life Chapman was plagued by debts and was eventually living in near-poverty. It seemed to begin in 1585 when Chapman was offered a bond of surety in order to obtain a loan. Chapman planned to use the proceeds to "use in Attendance upon the then Right Honorable Sir Rafe Sadler Knight". The surety was offered by John Wolfall.

Chapman's designs for Court were short-lived. It appears the money was never received but the papers had been signed and Wolfall used them to pursue Chapman for repayment for many years.

During the first part of the early 1590s Chapman was in Europe, in military action in the Low Countries fighting under the famed English general Sir Francis Vere.

It is from this period that his earliest published works are found including the obscure philosophical poems The Shadow of Night (1594) and Ovid's Banquet of Sense (1595).

By the end of the 1590s, Chapman had become a successful playwright, working for the Elizabethan Theatrical entrepreneur, Philip Henslowe, and later for the Children of the Chapel.

In 1600, Wolfall, still claiming his money, had Chapman arrested over the outstanding debt. In 1608 Wolfall's son, having inherited his father's papers, sued yet again, Chapman's only resort was to petition the Court of Chancery for equity.

To add insult to injury it also appears that Chapman had little time to train with Sadler although he seems present in the Sadler household from 1577–83, and dedicated all his Homerical translations to him.

From 1598 he published his translation of the Iliad in installments. In 1616 the complete Iliad and Odyssey appeared in The Whole Works of Homer, the first complete English translation, which until Alexander Pope's, was the most popular in the English language and was the entry point for most English readers of these magnificent poems.

Chapman does appear to have been diligent in obtaining another patron who would finance his growing reputation.

Robert Devereux, Second Earl of Essex seemed likely to be his patron before being executed for treason by Elizabeth I in 1601.

However Chapman was by now of some renown. It is often said that he worked with Shakespeare, and certainly, in the employment of Henslowe, that could well be an artistic or business relationship pushed upon him.

The great Ben Jonson was also using Chapman's talents in the play Eastward Ho (1605), co-written with John Marston. Both Chapman and Jonson landed in jail over some satirical references to the Scots in the play but both were quick to say that Marston was the culprit.

The friendship with Jonson later broke down, most probably as a result of Jonson's public feud with Inigo Jones. Some satiric, scathing lines, written at a point after the burning of Jonson's desk and papers, provide some evidence of the rift. The poem lampooning Jonson's aggressive behaviour and self-believed superiority remained unpublished during Chapman's lifetime; it was found in documents collected after his death.

Chapman had continued on his great translations of Homer's Iliad and the Odyssey for many years. He had begun their publication in installments starting in 1598. In 1612, his latest patron, Prince Henry, died at the age of eighteen of typhoid fever. He had promised Chapman £300 and a pension on their publication. Whilst publication in their entirety was some years away Chapman felt the money was his due and when the Estate neglected the commitment Chapman petitioned for the money owed him. The petition was ineffective.

Chapman's resultant poverty did not diminish his ability or his standing among the starried gallery of his fellow Elizabethan poets and dramatists.

His talents as a translator were unquestionable. His work on the Odyssey is written in iambic pentameter, and his Iliad in iambic heptameter. (The Greek original is in dactylic hexameter.) Chapman often extends and elaborates on Homer's original contents to add descriptive detail or moral and philosophical interpretation and emphasis.

These translations were very much admired both by those unable to read Greek but inquiring of Homer and by many artists themselves. John Keats, was reverential in his famous poem On First Looking into Chapman's Homer, and other poets from Samuel Taylor Coleridge to T. S. Eliot were equal in their admiration.

Chapman today is under-rated and woefully forgotten. His plays show a willingness to experiment with dramatic form: An Humorous Day's Mirth was one of the first plays to be written in the style of "humours comedy" which Ben Jonson later used. With The Widow's Tears, he was also one of the first writers to meld comedy with more serious themes and thus creating the tragicomedy.

Another interesting creative pursuit of these times was the writing and performance of masques, and they were perhaps regarded as the highest of art forms. Part of this accolade may well be because of the audience being specifically that of the Court and therefore more refined and sophisticated. Obviously with the Puritan's closing the theatres in 1642 and the onset of the Civil War masques ceased.

Chapman wrote one of the most successful masques of the Jacobean era, The Memorable Masque of the Middle Temple and Lincoln's Inn, performed on February 15th, 1613. Another masque, The Masque of the Twelve Months, performed on Twelfth Night 1619 is also now given as Chapman's.

Unfortunately due to their small audience and the cataclysmic events of the era little documentation has survived. What can be stated is that the form developed in various ways, initially in Italy. A masque involved music and dancing, singing and acting, with an elaborate stage design, in which the architectural framing and costumes might be designed by a renowned architect together with performances from professional actors and musicians.

To this other works are now being recognised as Chapman's hand. The lost plays The Fatal Love and A Yorkshire Gentlewoman And Her Son were assigned to Chapman in Stationers' Register entries in 1660. Both of these plays were among fifty or so used for kindling and other uses by the cook of the neglectful collector John Warburton. The lost play Christianetta (registered 1640) may have been a collaboration between Chapman and Richard Brome, or a revision by Brome of a Chapman work.

Other poems by Chapman include: De Guiana, Carmen Epicum (1596), on the exploits of Sir Walter Raleigh; a continuation of Christopher Marlowe's unfinished Hero and Leander (1598); and Euthymiae Raptus; or the Tears of Peace (1609). Some have considered Chapman to be the "rival poet" of Shakespeare's Sonnets.

In truth Chapman's known poetry was not particularly influential; his translations of Homer's Iliad and Odyssey, and the Homeric Batrachomyomachia undoubtedly were.

George Chapman died in London on May 12th, 1634 having lived his latter years in poverty and debt. He was buried at St Giles in the Fields. A monument to him designed by Inigo Jones marked his tomb, and stands today inside the church.

George Chapman – A Concise Bibliography

Plays – Comedies

The Blind Beggar of Alexandria (1596; printed 1598)
An Humorous Day's Mirth (1597; printed 1599)
All Fools (printed 1605)
Monsieur D'Olive (1605; printed 1606)
The Gentleman Usher (printed 1606)
May Day (printed 1611)
The Widow's Tears (printed 1612)

Plays – Tragedies
Bussy D'Ambois (1607)
The Conspiracy and Tragedy of Charles, Duke of Byron (1608)
The Revenge of Bussy D'Ambois (1613)
The Tragedy of Chabot, Admiral of France (published 1639).
Caesar and Pompey

Plays – Collaborations
Eastward Ho with Ben Johnson and John Marston (1605)

Plays – Attributed but not Completely Verified
The Fatal Love
A Yorkshire Gentlewoman and Her Son
Christianetta
Sir Gyles Goosecap

Masques
The Memorable Masque of the Middle Temple and Lincoln's Inn (Performed on 15 February 1613)
The Masque of the Twelve Months (Performed on Twelfth Night, 1619)

Translations
Homer's Iliad (1598-1616)
Homers Odyssey (1598-1616)
Homeric Hymns, the Georgics of Virgil, The Works of Hesiod (1618, dedicated to Francis Bacon),
The Hero and Leander of Musaeus (1618)
The Fifth Satire of Juvenal (1624).
Batrachomyomachia.

Poetry

George Chapman wrote several poems. Among his other poetical works are:-

De Guiana, Carmen Epicum (1596)
Hero and Leander (Begun by Marlowe Chapman continued with the work.

Euthymiae Raptus; or the Tears of Peace (1609)